P9-DMJ-113

# . . . AND THE CLIENTS WENT WILD!

# . . . AND THE CLIENTS WENT WILD!

## How Savvy Professionals Win All the Business They Want

### MARIBETH KUZMESKI

WILEY

JOHN WILEY & SONS, INC.

Copyright © 2010 by Maribeth Kuzmeski. All rights reserved.

Published by John Wiley & Sons, Inc., Hoboken, New Jersey.
Published simultaneously in Canada.

No part of this publication may be reproduced, stored in a retrieval system, or transmitted in any form or by any means, electronic, mechanical, photocopying, recording, scanning, or otherwise, except as permitted under Section 107 or 108 of the 1976 United States Copyright Act, without either the prior written permission of the Publisher, or authorization through payment of the appropriate per-copy fee to the Copyright Clearance Center, Inc., 222 Rosewood Drive, Danvers, MA 01923, (978) 750-8400, fax (978) 646-8600, or on the web at www.copyright.com. Requests to the Publisher for permission should be addressed to the Permissions Department, John Wiley & Sons, Inc., 111 River Street, Hoboken, NJ 07030, (201) 748-6011, fax (201) 748-6008, or online at http://www.wiley.com/go/permissions.

Limit of Liability/Disclaimer of Warranty: While the publisher and author have used their best efforts in preparing this book, they make no representations or warranties with respect to the accuracy or completeness of the contents of this book and specifically disclaim any implied warranties of merchantability or fitness for a particular purpose. No warranty may be created or extended by sales representatives or written sales materials. The advice and strategies contained herein may not be suitable for your situation. You should consult with a professional where appropriate. Neither the publisher nor author shall be liable for any loss of profit or any other commercial damages, including but not limited to special, incidental, consequential, or other damages.

For general information on our other products and services or for technical support, please contact our Customer Care Department within the United States at (800) 762-2974, outside the United States at (317) 572-3993 or fax (317) 572-4002.

Wiley also publishes its books in a variety of electronic formats. Some content that appears in print may not be available in electronic books. For more information about Wiley products, visit our web site at www.wiley.com.

**Library of Congress Cataloging-in-Publication Data:**
Kuzmeski, Maribeth.
    And the clients went wild!: how savvy professionals win all the business they want/ Maribeth Kuzmeski.
       p. cm.
    Includes index.
    ISBN 978-0-470-60176-1 (cloth)
    ISBN 978-0-470-76988-1 (ebk)
    ISBN 978-0-470-76989-8 (ebk)
    ISBN 978-0-470-76990-4 (ebk)
    1. Customer services.    2. Success in business.    I. Title.
    HF5415.5.K89 2010
    658.8—dc22                                                    2010005940

Printed in the United States of America

10  9  8  7  6  5  4  3  2

To my children Elizabeth and Shane—your energy
and love keep me moving!

# CONTENTS

# ACKNOWLEDGMENTS

I am grateful for everyone who has helped me take this book from concept to reality. A special thank you to my family for supporting me and my long hours writing and researching. To my parents for giving me the background, love, and experiences that have ultimately led to what I do today. To my clients who have given me many successes to write about, and to all of those who agreed to be interviewed for this book. To my publisher, John Wiley & Sons, Inc., and the key people there who have believed in my books—Richard Narramore and Matt Holt. To my developmental editor Christine Moore and production editor Lauren Freestone at John Wiley & Sons, Inc., as well as their marketing team. To my literary agent Jay Poynor who has enabled my writing to get published. And to Dottie DeHart and her public relations team at DeHart and Company. Finally, a special thank you to my readers, followers, and advocates—without you all of this would be a big secret.

Aclyio!

# INTRODUCTION

Businesses, business owners, and professionals—as well as sports teams and politicians—purposely reach out for people's recognition and affirmation that they have *what others want*. Some entities have gained elite status and positive exposure beyond their wildest dreams because they have possessed exactly what people need or desire. This kind of exposure by those who know them best—their clients, fans, and constituents—has loudly proclaimed their worth.

But getting clients to literally "go wild" about you and what you do is—for most businesspeople—slightly more elusive. First, there must be some attribute worth going wild *about*. Then, you have to reach out to find those who may be interested in your message and offering. Clients don't randomly stumble on a business; smart companies communicate with a target audience, in the hopes they are listening and liking and buying.

This act of reaching out is marketing.

The American Marketing Association's official definition of marketing is, "the activity, set of institutions, and processes for creating, communicating, delivering, and exchanging offerings that have value for customers, clients, partners, and society at large."

In other words, marketing is about attracting qualified buyers to your products or services.

There have been hundreds of thousands of books and articles written about marketing tactics, new and traditional strategies, ideas and formulas to use in your business to attract clients, convince them to buy, and then get them to do it (buy) again. But when you cut through all of it, you'll find that the concept of marketing is really much simpler than all the definitions and words written on the topic. In fact, after spending more than two decades working in marketing in a variety of different industries—including politics, sports, and technology, and the past 15 years in financial services—I have developed my own definition of marketing:

*Marketing is the act of creating a compelling message for an offering that clients will buy and then won't be able to stop talking about.*

It is not about implementing a hundred new tactics for reaching your target audience and hoping that one hits the target. It is about finding and using just a few strategies *well*.

## Tapping into the Emotional Connection

In order to truly get clients to go wild about your business, there must be an overriding and strong emotional connection; the same kind that you feel when you cheer for your favorite sports team, or support a cause that means something to you. You can get others to connect to your company, product, or service by emotionally energizing them through a passionate delivery of information. This is a true differentiator, because so few people and businesses actually act with this kind of enthusiasm. Thus, when someone is exhibiting passion about something, you take notice.

In my previous book, *The Connectors* (John Wiley & Sons, Inc., 2009), I wrote about how critically important it is to connect with others in business to fulfill your potential, create enormous opportunities, and gain personal success. But to take a step beyond being a connector is to define the specifics that will turn connections into sales, and buyers into fans. The relationship you develop with others is what creates this possibility. It is only when you tap into emotional bonds that people will truly "love you" and go wild about what you do.

Tapping into others' emotions requires that you elicit something called an "emotional convention" in the minds of those you want to buy from you. This happens when the seven basic factors—depicted in Figure I.1—

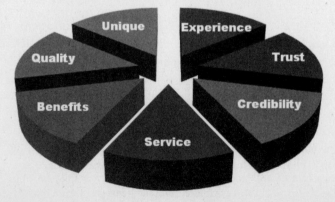

**Emotional Convention**

Unique
Experience
Quality
Trust
Benefits
Credibility
Service

Figure I.1   The Seven Factors in the Emotional Convention

come together to form a powerful, undeniable sentiment. The convention is ultimately the agreement between your conscious and subconscious mind to accept the merits and value of a certain person, company, or offering. If successful, the emotional convention results in an "I'm wild about you" conclusion.

## The Seven Factors in the Emotional Convention

The underlying focus throughout this book will be on these seven emotional convention factors. Unless you are able to combine these elements for clients, there will be little chance of an emotional bond. And unless you can reach an exceptional level for each of them, the kind of raving fans you desire will likely not materialize.

1. Quality
2. Experience
3. Benefits
4. Service
5. Trust
6. Credibility
7. Unique

So—have you tapped into the emotional convention in the minds of your prospects and clients? If you haven't experienced an overwhelming response of loyalty and consistent buying habits from your clients, then you may want to take the emotional convention assessment below to determine what may be missing.

A rating that is anywhere from 32 to 35 will bring you the kind of emotional buy-in that's needed to create the intense loyalty necessary to get your clients going wild. It is more critical than ever in business today to establish strong, genuine connections between businesses and clients. Without them, the product or service is lost in a sea of noise and similar offerings.

## Creating Unconditional Client Loyalty

Sporting events and teams often display this kind of emotional connection between teams and their fans; some that have been built over generations. As the Green Bay Packers state in their NFL Films introduction to

---

## Emotional Convention Assessment

Rate yourself or your business on a scale of 1–5 with 5 being the best.

*Am I providing* . . .

1. Quality products or services?       ⑤ ④ ③ ② ①

2. A memorable experience for my clients?    ⑤ ④ ③ ② ①

3. Benefits they want or need?       ⑤ ④ ③ ② ①

4. Service that meets or exceeds expectations? ⑤ ④ ③ ② ①

5. Trust in products, services, and us?     ⑤ ④ ③ ② ①

6. Proven credibility?       ⑤ ④ ③ ② ①

7. Something unique?       ⑤ ④ ③ ② ①

---

the team, there is an "unbreakable bond between football generations." I certainly am a case study of this football loyalty, having learned about the game and what it means to be a fan from my football-loving grandmother. I cheered for our team when they were terrible, and basked in the glow of the wins when they were better. But I never considered moving to another; *this* was my team. Fan loyalty is an emotional connection that's often stronger than any other loyalty, frequently due to these generational or family-based connections.

So how can businesses create this same type of unconditional loyalty? How can they elicit allegiance that is so strong that it continues on—even when the team loses or performs poorly year after year? How can you form an emotional bond that causes you to be more likely to forgive and forget than you would for a company that makes a mistake or sells a product of poor quality?

The only way to win this kind of devotion from your clients is to establish an emotional connection between you and them. It's truly based on how you have made them feel.

## The Goal of This Book

This book's primary goal is to give you the blueprint for cultivating loyal clients and generating growing sales through a collection of case studies, principles, and tactics that have proven successful for others. Ultimately, this blueprint is designed to trigger the emotional convention in the minds of prospects and clients—followed by a response that is so powerful that your loyal clients won't be able to stop talking about you.

## CHAPTER 1

# Executive Summary

## The Five Core Principles for Turning Clients and Prospects into Raving Fans

"Perfect clients" are those who will pay for the full value of your product or services, rave about what you do, and go wild for anything that you offer. Lots of businesses have *good* clients, but only an elite few have passionate, loyal, vocal clients. This type of client is one that not only keeps coming back for more, but also finds the need to share you with family, friends, and even strangers. Perfect clients are often what drive a firm's explosive growth. And although the perfect client is found only in a perfect world (which doesn't exist), there are many businesses that can enjoy the enthusiasm of the *nearly* perfect passion of their clients.

I have observed companies large and small through the eyes of my consulting firm; conducted extensive research; and read literally thousands of business books in search of commonalities and concepts for repeatable professional success. I have ultimately been searching, as many of us are, for the "secret sauce" that some businesses have mixed together to create incremental success. And although I am trained in marketing—and this *is* a marketing book—it is not one that lists or explains the basic concepts and textbook theories of marketing approaches. It is instead filled with the lessons and premises of a variety of business success stories—many that have never been heard before—to illustrate effective and unique strategies for attracting loyal fans and advocates.

There is no shortcut to obtaining success. No amount of marketing budget can get people to love you. Spending money is *truly* overrated; thoughtful strategy is not. People nowadays are far less likely to become loyal, given the overwhelming noise of the countless marketing messages they face. The objective is to get clients into the game—*your* game. And to accomplish this feat in today's "new media" world, businesses are being forced to change. This has never been more evident, as many of the largest companies are no longer only measuring advertising return on investment. In fact marketing today is being measured by taking into account the crucial free media and word-of-mouth efforts, as well as traditional strategies. Success simply doesn't come the way it used to.

Businesses that have effectively created a loyal following of passionate and vocal clients have followed some, if not all, of *five fundamental marketing principles*. When you adopt even some of these principles you can bring more success to your business and a following of clients who simply go wild for what you do.

In Part I—"The Principles," of this book, I go over each of these five principles in detail. The following is a summary of the principles for marketing success.

## First Principle

### What Are *You* Doing that No One Else Is Doing? *Build Client Delight Through Differentiation*

In order to gain exposure, it certainly helps to be unique or offer something unique—or do something that no one else dares. And although standing out from the crowd definitely gets people excited, it is probably the riskiest of the five principles. However, it is perhaps equally risky to run a conservative, under-the-radar firm today that may just cause you to become something of the past. Instead, successful firms find ways to be *so* exciting—while sticking with their values—that people don't have a choice but to pay attention . . . and buy. In Chapter 2, "First Principle," examples of companies that truly stand out in the market include a gas station, a printer, and a toy store, as well as a multilevel marketing firm for men only, and a rubber duck company. *Really.*

## Second Principle

### Focus Your Marketing on Benefits, Results, and a Call to Action
*What's Really in it for Them*

People don't buy features—they buy the benefits of those features. In fact, to make it even more clear, people buy *results*. There is a significant lack of clarity surrounding what businesses sell, however. People rarely make buying decisions based on all the features of a product or service, yet that's what most businesses promote over and over again. Many companies just assume that their customers *know* what the benefits are, and exactly why to buy their product or service. They leave it up to the prospect to figure out the benefits. Many businesses make the mistake of emphasizing features. Examples of companies that have focused successfully on their benefits and included a strong call to action include a hotel, a "sales hunter" firm, a beverage company, and a card store, which are highlighted in Chapter 3, "Second Principle."

## Third Principle

### Go Viral!
*Create Memorable Impactful Messaging Worthy of a Pass-Along*

At its core, viral marketing is about the rapid spread of a way of thinking about a product or service—and how it affects those interested. It generates exponential growth in a message's exposure and impact, and has proven to far outperform the results that other types marketing produce. In Chapter 4, "Third Principle," you can read about companies that have created profitable viral marketing campaigns that have transferred into extraordinary impact and sales, including a book, a government, a search engine, a nonprofit, a film—and even guitar lessons.

## Fourth Principle

### Leverage Your Business Network for Incremental Growth
*Find and Cultivate Centers of Influence to Move Your Message Fast*

Thankfully for salespeople everywhere, strategies for leveraging *themselves* exist as well! It takes a plan, but putting current relationships to work can be the miracle answer to the typical grind of cold calls and prospecting for new business. Advocates, centers of influence, and clients will give you referrals and introductions that are critical to expanding your reach and incremental sales growth. But who wants to connect you with others? Lots of people do; it simply takes finding out what's in it for them. In Chapter 5, "Fourth Principle," there are specific examples of successful leveraging strategies employed by a child author, a spa, a real estate agent, a QVC star, and a salesperson.

## Fifth Principle

### The Critical Importance of Execution in Your Game Plan
*Good Execution Is Better than Good Strategy*

In today's fast-moving, completely networked world, superior execution is clearly driving success for business. Small business owners are great at adopting many new marketing ideas; what they are not so great at is finishing. The best marketing strategy is the one you can pull off completely.

Think of it this way: Any marketing strategy you choose—and stay with until it's executed fully and with precision—is actually the best marketing method for you. It is the execution that makes a good strategy look great. Examples of great execution include football, a speaker and author, an accounting firm, and an insurance company.

The next five chapters provide a complete description and examples of how to use the five fundamental marketing principles. Then, in Part II—"The Playbook," you find 13 chapters filled with online and traditional marketing techniques that are working today. I also provide you with a template that you can use to structure a complete marketing and action plan.

# The Principles

# First Principle
# What Are You Doing that
# No One Else Is Doing?

## Build Client Delight Through
## Your Differentiation

Today your products and services often require a Herculean effort to gain exposure. With all the noise in your clients' and potential clients' daily lives, it certainly hasn't become any *easier* to attract attention and appeal to your target market. But it has never been more critical for business survival.

Often you have to step outside of the current norms and stand out to attract attention. But in order to be noticed in a credible way, you must have a compelling reason for grabbing people's attention. Your product, promotion, offer, staff, or culture—or something else about your business—must be unique in some way. As mentioned in Chapter 1, "Executive Summary," running a conservative, under-the-radar firm today may cause you to become something of the past. Successful firms need to find ways to be exciting, while sticking with their values, so that people will pay attention—and buy.

## A Gas Station with a Cult Following

Sometimes what your competitors consider to be "unimportant" may just turn out to be the differentiation that gets customers coming back for more. For example, how does a Texas-based gas station chain get patrons talking about them all over the world? It's simple: by having something that people rarely find at gas stations. And by providing customers with what others don't, these chains have become something of a roadside tourist attraction.

Throughout Texas, Buc-ee's gas stations have focused their number-one offering on what people dread most about stopping at a gas station: the bathrooms! Each of the 30 Buc-ee's locations has incredibly clean, substantially sized bathrooms, along with full-time attendants to keep them in tip-top shape. Buc-ee's built its entire business around the bathrooms—a feature the company knew it could use to differentiate its business. The idea behind this strategy is that if motorists pull in to use the restroom, they are likely to buy. Buc-ee's employs more than 1,000 Texans, has been written about in local newspapers, and has even been featured on national TV. An ABC news segment about Buc-ee's told the story of drivers waiting hundreds of miles to stop at a gas station—essentially planning their entire trip around their stop at the next Buc-ee's!

Buc-ee's co-owner Beaver Aplin said he gets hundreds of e-mails expressing customers' appreciation monthly. "A soldier in Iraq wrote that he slapped a Buc-ee's beaver logo sticker on his tank," Aplin said. "In our industry you don't expect someone to send fan mail about a gas station. It makes you feel good." See Figure 2.1.

But Buc-ee's doesn't rely just on word of mouth to spread the word about its gas stations. Billboards cover the roads in Texas, promoting their best-known attribute: the bathrooms. For instance, the billboards read,

**Figure 2.1    Buc-ee's**
*Source*: www.bucees.com.

"Only 262 Miles to Buc-ee's. You can hold it." The company also has its own blog where it requests and promotes pictures on its web site, in the media, and in its advertising, as well as customer testimonials like:

*Whether [it's] because it reminds me of the schlocky roadside souvenir stops of my youth, or due to its winsome beaver logo, I'm smitten with a chain of South Texas convenience stores called Buc-ee's. Seriously, I love this place so much that if I weren't already married, I'd have my wedding there.*

—Jacquielynn Floyd, *Dallas Morning News Metro* blogger

*Better than Wal-Mart and McDonalds all wound up together! It's a mini-Bass Pro Shop with a toy store for kids and adults.*

—Tabitha, from "East TX around Lufkin"

*The Buc-ee's T-shirt opens doors. I [wore mine when I] stopped by Amy's Ice Cream in San Antonio and as I walked in . . . the counter staff [members yelled], "Buc-ee's!" I got free ice cream: Ancho Chocolate and Chocolate Guiness.*

—Anonymous fan

What do people dislike most about your industry, service, or product offering? For example, the bathrooms at gas stations.

_____
_____
_____
_____

Can you offer a solution to what people dislike most?

_____
_____
_____
_____

What can you provide that is truly different?

_____
_____
_____
_____

## When the Offer Is Surprising, People Pay Attention!

If you offer something of real value for free, people will listen. In fact, "free" can convert price shoppers into loyal customers. This is the model that online print company Vistaprint used to convert a typical commodity service—printing—into a company that generated more than $500 million in revenue in 2009.

"We wanted to create scale by blowing our customers away with jaw-dropping value," said the company's public relations manager Jeff Esposito. "So we came up with an offer for free business cards."

The offer has a certain appeal to their target market: small businesses. These companies need printing, but they're often cost-conscious customers. So Vistaprint offers 250 business cards for free, with a nominal $5.67 shipping and processing charge.

Vistaprint services more than 8 million small businesses and consumers annually by offering products for the home and office. The company has a unique model supported by proprietary technologies, high-volume production facilities, and direct marketing expertise. Its offerings range from business cards, brochures, and web sites to invitations, thank-you notes, and calendars. As a global company, Vistaprint employs more than 1,850 people, and ships to more than 120 countries.

"The free cards we print have a small promotion printed on the bottom that reads, 'Business Cards are free at Vistaprint.com,'" said Esposito. "If a customer wants to pay for the cards, then they won't have the promotion on the bottom."

That same promotional message began popping up in various places, which allowed the offer to find viral travel on the Internet and among businesses. "When you offer a huge value proposition, it speaks for itself!" Esposito said. Today, 66 percent of Vistaprint's business comes from returning customers. In the first quarter of FY 2010, the company acquired 1.4 million new customers—many who started with a free order.

---

List an offering you could make that would surprise customers (and maybe even go viral)!

_____

_____

_____

_____

# Is "Free" Really Such a Good Offer?

Companies typically take the traditional approach of offering their products or services to customers for a price. It's a simple and straightforward way of doing business—I provide you with something and, in turn, you pay me for it. But like Vistaprint, more and more savvy businesses today enjoy dramatic success by offering some of their goods and services for free.

Free offerings are becoming an increasingly popular indirect route to revenue. For instance, some cellular companies will give away a phone if you sign a two-year service contract. DirecTV and other satellite television services give the satellite dish to customers for free in order to get the paid subscription to the programming. Google gives away their main service—Internet search—and are in turn able to earn revenue from advertisements and paid searches. Every time you do a search on Google, you see its Sponsored Links; and whenever you click on one of those links, Google charges the web site a fee for the click. You'll notice advertising from Google on various other web sites that you visit—something Google calls AdSense in which they charge a fee to these sites—part of which is given to the webmaster who publishes the ads. However, the majority of their offerings are free.

Chris Anderson presents the premise in his book *Free* (Hyperion, July 2009) that there is a generational and global shift at play in which customers insist on free goods. Anderson claims that those below the age of 30 refuse to pay for information that they know will eventually be available somewhere for free. In countries like China, piracy accounts for about 95 percent of music consumption—something that may sound to some like an equally terrible and terrifying fact. However, artists and music labels in China—who profit from free publicity through their concerts and merchandising—welcome music piracy.

Some businesses are beginning to offer what is often referred to as a "freemium" (a word that's created by combining the two aspects of the business model, "free" and "premium")[1]: a business model that works by offering basic Web services or a downloadable digital product for free[2] while charging a premium for advanced or special features.[3] Red Zone Marketing offers many freemium products, downloads, and online courses in order to give people who will only meet with the firm online a chance to experience the kind of value the company provides. Red Zone Marketing gives this material away in the hopes that potential customers like what they see—find themselves wanting more at some point.

What "freemium" could you offer?

_____

_____

_____

_____

## Focus on Differentiating with Your People

How does a business grow without any advertising, salespeople, or participation at industry events and tradeshows? By doing things a little bit differently, and with a lot of passion.

The Bargains Group in Toronto, Canada, is a discount wholesaler of promotional business products, family clothing, accessories, gifts, toys, bedding and linen, personal hygiene products, and tradeshow promotional materials. The group procures clearance wholesale items for customers across Canada based on supply and demand. The company is ready to fulfill customers' needs for everything from 10,000 medical promotional items to 50 custom embroidered ball caps—all at deeply discounted prices.

Jody Steinhauer began The Bargains Group in 1988 from her kitchen table by purchasing a variety of different clothing and reselling it to discount clothing stores. Today, she runs a multimillion-dollar firm with more than 4,000 different items for sale. The most unique aspect of the company is its employees.

"We offer what we call 'branding at a bargain' for the businesses we work with. Each team member truly pays attention to our client businesses," said Steinhauer. "We work with them to sell *their* products and get them out the door."

Although many firms advertise how "different" their people are, or how they focus on service, The Bargain Group actually *proves* this assertion. The company doesn't advertise or employ salespeople, yet manages to make millions of dollars selling their products, so it must be doing *something* right, and certainly something unique. Sure, the company offers inexpensive products that occasionally have viral appeal by virtue of their low cost. However, for a small firm with only 20 employees, the bargain basement approach can't be *all* there is—because there is undoubtedly some company somewhere that can offer better prices. So what makes the difference?

"We focus on hiring fun, vivacious people with [a focus on] a culture of service," said Steinhauer. "We hire those [who] have had a service job in another industry; for instance, a receptionist at a hair salon. The results are that we do what others only say they will do—we actually service our customers personally. We don't even have voicemail. Our people are the real differentiator, and the reason we don't do any advertising or have never gone to the industry standard trade shows. Word just travels about us!"

---

Who do you hire? What type of person do you *want* to hire?

_____

_____

_____

_____

---

## If No One Is Doing It—Should You?

Here's an idea: How about starting a Tupperware-type party for men only with a complete set of "Man Laws"—meat and beer essentials, and discussions about grilling. And the advisors don't host parties, they host "Meatings." A home run, right—because no one else is doing it?

Well, it's been a home run so far for a couple of Midwestern twenty-somethings who started the first "home party" direct sales business designed for men called Man Cave. Man Cave is not a leader in its industry—it *is* the industry! For years, thousands of companies have demonstrated and sold products to groups of women in their homes. Man Cave does it now for men.

Nick Beste, 22, of Minnesota, and Kevin Carlow, 24, of Wisconsin, started the company as a male-only alternative to female-centric success stories from organizations like Silpada, Tupperware, and Partylite. Man Cave has grown from having three advisors in summer 2009, to exploding in growth of advisors and revenues. In fact, said, cofounder Carlow, "We anticipate crossing over $3 million by November 2010."

Man Cave advisors market the company's products primarily through a male-only gathering referred to as a MEATing. The advisors receive commission payments based on their own sales, in addition to the sales of the team they have recruited to also sell Man Cave products. "It's a good excuse to hang out with the guys, drink a few beers, eat some brats and—most importantly—learn some new techniques about grilling," said Beste.

After a person decides to host a MEATing, he invites others to attend. A Man Cave advisor attends and brings an ample supply of free premium meat—including steaks, chicken, and brats. A MEATing can revolve around a grilling demonstration, poker tournaments, a sporting event—or any other reason guys can come up with to hang out with one another.

"This is the best feature of a Man Cave MEATing," said Beste. "Besides viewing our product line, you eat hearty at the party."

Unlike at other home parties, there are no formal presentations, just products to sample and view. The group sells meat, grilling products, marinades, as well as poker-playing items and apparel. And they promote their Man Laws that dictate that—of course—"Grilling, regardless of weather, is always the first choice for cooking."

---

What product or service could you provide that no one else has taken to market?

_____

_____

_____

_____

---

## What Will People Buy?

Entrepreneurs frequently speculate on what people might be willing to buy. Some conduct extensive research; more look for obvious gaps in offerings; and others simply go with their "gut feelings." But there are a few entrepreneurs that just throw caution to the wind, and create a brand new category.

"I knew from day one that if the concept was unique enough and given enough time, it would definitely find its market . . . and it did!" said Craig Wolfe, president of CelebriDucks—a company that produces a line of celebrity rubber ducks that are fashioned after some icons of film, music, athletics, and history. They have produced CelebriDuck likenesses of Elvis Presley, Marilyn Monroe, The Wizard of Oz, James Dean, KISS, Barack Obama, James Brown, The Blues Brothers, Mr. T, and Shakespeare. To date, they have created more than 200 different CelebriDucks—and have pioneered an entirely new collectible.

The company has received a tremendous amount of publicity. Their products have been featured on networks including NBC, Fox, CBS, CNN, ABC, Showtime, ESPN, VH1, TNT, A&E; and specifically, television shows like *Late Night with Conan O'Brien*, *The Tonight Show with Jay Leno*, and *Jimmy Kimmel Live*. The company has been written about in articles in *Sports Illustrated*, *U.S. News and World Report*, *ESPN The Magazine*, *Maxim*, the *New York Times*, *USA Today*, the *Los Angeles Times*, *San*

*Francisco Chronicle, Toronto Sun, Playboy,* the *Chicago Sun Times,* and *Fortune Small Business.*

ESPN.com recently ran a poll for the fan's favorite stadium giveaway in which CelebriDucks beat out Beanie Babies, bobblehead dolls, Pez dispensers, and Matchbox cars. CelebriDucks have been used by numerous teams in the NBA, NHL, and MLB—such as the New York Yankees, the Philadelphia 76ers, the Houston Rockets, the Chicago Cubs, and countless others. The company sells its Blues Brother's ducks at all House of Blues venues nationwide. And Gorton Seafood—one of the largest frozen fish companies in the United States—did a four-month national promotion with the creation of a duck of the Gorton Fisherman, which enjoyed tremendous success. Not only did the ducks sell out, the promotion was the most profitable in the company's history.

---

Can you create an entirely new category?

_____

_____

_____

_____

---

## Stand Out with Your Promotion—Take a Risk!

"Our city and state have been hit hard by the economy over the past 18 months," said Phil Wrzesinski, owner of Jackson, Michigan–based toy store Toy House. "Our unemployment [rate has been] hovering around 15 to 16 percent for the past several months, [and] our schools, countywide, have lost over 800 students this year. In a county of only 150,000, that is a significant number of people who have left town. I also have to compete locally with a Wal-Mart, a Toys "R" Us, a Target, two Kmarts, and two Meijer's. Yet because of our [radio] promotions, we have seen a steady increase in both loyalty and sales. In fact, my toy sales are *up* over previous years!"

Since Toy House began their radio campaign in 2005—using ads like "The Men's Bathroom" (script below)—they have seen a steady increase in both loyalty and sales. You can listen to all of their radio ads at www .toyhouseonline.com/radio.html. "In August 2008, we ran an ad on our local radio station that created a huge buzz that was talked about for a whole year," said Wrzesinski. "We had the local DJs wondering what was in the men's bathroom. We had droves of customers coming in to see what was in the men's bathroom. We even had other media outlets speculating on what was in the men's bathroom. My wife was approached on the street and asked about it, and our employees were hounded outside of work, too." And here's why:

> *I couldn't believe it. They were taking customers into the men's bathroom. Yes, my staff was taking men and women, young and old into our men's bathroom. And the customers were coming out laughing and giggling, oh yeah, and buying, too. I guess when you find a product that cool, you just have to show it off however and wherever you can. (laugh) The men's bathroom, gotta love it. Toy House in downtown Jackson. We're here to make you smile.*
>
> —Men's Bathroom Radio Ad Script

The product in question is a night light in the shape of either a turtle or ladybug (called the Twilight Ladybug and Twilight Turtle, and designed by a company called Cloud B), which projects stars onto the ceiling and walls of a darkened room. Although it was designed as a night light for infants and toddlers, Toy House sells just as many to kids of all ages—and even adults. However, the only way for employees to show it off was in the dark confines of the Toy House's men's bathroom.

What was especially impressive was that people were still talking about the ad—even months after it stopped running. "A customer came in six months after the ad stopped running, and asked what was in the men's bathroom. He explained that the whole conversation at the Christmas dinner table centered on what was going on in our men's bathroom."

Just recently, the DJ at the local radio station on which Toy House advertises came in and bought one of its night lights. He was complaining that his three-and-a-half-year-old child would not go to sleep or stay asleep at night. "This morning, he broke the secret of the men's bathroom wide open [by telling his audience about the product]—because his child slept through the entire night without incident!" said Wrzesinski.

According to Wrzesinski, an independent toy store that sells 24 of a particular item is called a good seller, while selling 72 or more makes it a "hot item." "We have now sold over 1,200 Twilight Ladybugs and Turtles thanks to this promotion," said Wrzesinski.

---

What are you selling that you could promote in a unique way?

_____

_____

_____

## Offer Something that No One Else Will

James Dillard, owner of Dillard's Septic Service in Annapolis, Maryland, runs a business that most others might consider "beneath" them. Yet Dillard earns a six-figure income doing what some would call mundane, boring, or downright disgusting. An October 10, 2007, article in *USA Today* by Del Jones entitled, "A Dirty Job, But Someone has to Get Rich Doing It," featured Dillard and other business owners who have entered into careers that many others simply would not. And it is a potential avenue for business owners who are looking for a way to generate more income.

Dillard works in a smelly business, but told *USA Today* that he goes most days without getting a splash on his clothes. "The only odor you catch is when you take off the cap and agitate the solids," he said.

Really!

In the Forbes 400 list of the wealthiest Americans for 2009, less than glamorous fields and products—including discount tires, roofing, salsa, lumber, and tequila—have produced extraordinary income. You might not consider these to be material that would create such great wealth, but each of these business owners found their niche and their differentiation, and their clients—*lots* of them—stood up and took notice!

What can you offer (or do) that no one else will?

_____

_____

_____

_____

### Take 15 and Get Your Clients Going Wild!
*A 15-Minute Client-Builder Exercise*

List a different approach or offer what no one else is doing.

_____

_____

_____

_____

## CHAPTER 3

# Second Principle
# Focus Your Marketing on Benefits, Results, and a Call to Action

## What's Really in It for Them

*When you try to sell the features of your product or service, you're making the customer do all the work to figure out why they want the feature.*

The biggest mistake people make in marketing—and a reason they find success to be so elusive—is not clearly explaining what the company is selling. Consumers rarely make buying decisions based on a product or service's features, yet that's what most businesses promote over and over again. People don't buy features; they buy the benefits that those features offer. In fact, to make it even more clear: people buy *results*. Many businesses assume that their customers know what the benefits are, and exactly why to buy their product or service. They leave it up to the prospect to derive their benefits. However, focusing on the features is a mistake that most businesses make.

What is the difference between a feature and benefit? Often, there is much confusion between the two.

*Definition of Features.* Features are *factual* statements about— often distinctive characteristics of—a product or service. Features are a means of providing benefits to customers; for instance, "Open 24 Hours" is a feature.

*Definition of Benefits.* Benefits are *value* statements about the feature of a product or service, with an emphasis on what the customer *gets*. A benefit answers the question, "Why should I care?" For instance, a benefit tells you that you should care because the product will make you look slimmer, help you close more sales, save lots of money on gas, or tastes great.

## Are Your Clients Making the Right Assumptions?

Approach your own product or service as if you'd never seen it. Then ask yourself—and anyone else who will answer—"What results will that feature bring me?" or "Why would I want to consider buying or switching?" You need to put yourself in the buyer's shoes, because whenever you act from your own point of view, you fill in the blanks with assumptions. Can your prospects do that? No matter what type of business you have, you think it's great because you fully understand it. But a prospect usually knows little or nothing about your offerings, and isn't able to make the same assumptions that you would.

Additionally, many businesses are too soft on their benefits. A soft benefit is similar to a glorified feature. These don't move people to act or remind them why they need to buy now. When you try to sell your product or service on features alone, you're making the customer do all the work, and figure out why they want the feature. It's in a seller's best interest to draw the connection for the prospective buyer.

*Example: LED Lightbulb*

Feature: Long-lasting bulb

Soft Benefit: Energy efficient and money-saving

Compelling Benefit: Uses up to 75 percent less energy than regular bulbs; lasts up to 10 times longer; reduces your electric bill.

*Example: Trump International Hotel & Tower*

Feature: A five-star property

Soft Benefit: The hotel offers excellent, five-star service

Compelling Benefit: The hotel treats you like you are a celebrity by rushing to take care of everything—from water to quench your thirst, to requesting to press your luggage-crushed suit for free. When you enter, any need you can think of is taken care of until you leave.

*Example: Financial Advisor*

Feature: Experienced financial professional with CFP and CFA licenses

Soft Benefit: Has a high level of expertise to help you make smart money decisions

Compelling Benefit: Will proactively be there for you to help you protect your assets and avoid making bad financial decisions. You will be able to truly enjoy the money you have earned in your life without worrying about investments.

## Finding the Compelling Benefits

Compelling benefits answer the question, "Why should I care?" But do you even know what your clients truly care about? And do your marketing messages address this?

---

What do your best clients want? What results do they *care* about?

_____

_____

_____

_____

---

---

### List How You Promote Your Products and Services Now

| Product or Service | Feature | Compelling Benefit |
|---|---|---|
| _____ | _____ | _____ |
| _____ | _____ | _____ |
| _____ | _____ | _____ |
| _____ | _____ | _____ |

---

## Pinning Down the Real Compelling Benefit

One of the problems in figuring out the truly compelling benefits of your product or service may be flexibility, because if you list what you consider to be the true benefits of your product, you may be missing a critical element. Therefore, it's best to list benefits based on what your *customers*— not you—believe is valuable. Sometimes what once was a benefit to someone really isn't, and those that should be aren't presented as such.

For instance, when the economy is booming and people have more expendable income, price is usually less important, and value more so. But when people are watching every penny they spend due to a change in their economic situations, the tables have turned—and price may all of a sudden become a vital feature. You have to constantly evaluate your benefits to avoid surprises. Your product or service may be the best on the market, but will people buy? Have you asked your clients and prospects?

---

Evaluate whether your clients and prospects *truly* care about your compelling benefits.

_____

_____

_____

_____

---

### It's All About the Results

Once you refocus, you realize that I'm really talking about *results*. So what are the ultimate outcomes of the features you offer your clients?

---

## List Your Current Features and Beside Each List the Result

| Feature | Result |
| --- | --- |
| | |
| | |
| | |
| | |
| | |

---

## Advertising Feelings

The late Charles Revlon—cosmetics executive and founder/CEO of Revlon Cosmetics—had the right answer: "In our factory, we make lipstick. In our advertising, we sell hope." And Theodore "Ted" Levitt, longtime economics professor at Harvard Business School and marketing expert, echoed that sentiment when he pointed out that, "Kodak sells film, but they don't advertise film. They advertise memories." In fact, there are many companies that have the confidence to stand up with their benefit alone. Harley-Davidson doesn't advertise bikes, they advertise the ride: "It's the sound of life getting bigger."

## Turning Benefits into Sales

Building business is not about making a lot of sales calls; it's about finding and connecting your product or service with the decision makers who want to buy. Dubbed "The Chief Door Opener," Caryn Kopp of Kopp Consulting has developed a streamlined, efficient process for developing companies that saves her clients countless hours, and brings dramatic success in a majority of cases.

The nationwide sales executives at Kopp Consulting focus with laser-like accuracy on the most important aspects of marketing a business. They are "sales hunters" who reach out to prospects armed with clear messaging of compelling benefits designed to open doors for businesses. Kopp has hired some of the best corporate salespeople—most of whom have 15 or more years of selling experience and success—who become a virtual sales force for the companies that Kopp represents. These sales experts help their clients identify key decision makers that have a need for their service and money to spend. They then create the messaging in language designed to be so relevant and compelling that prospects are quickly engaged and look forward to the initial meeting. They also develop a well-prepared list of answers to potential objections, so that a door is fully opened for their client companies.

"Messaging is the key," explained founder Caryn Kopp. "We help to create, define, and refine the exact messaging for clients, so that the prospect feels that they might regret it if they don't at least schedule a first appointment to find out more."

And the results are staggering. By communicating clear benefits and targets, Kopp Consulting is able to open the closed doors to large prospective buyers for their clients—who range from promotional products firms to video production companies.

Too good to be true? Well, success always comes at a price, but many of Kopp Consulting's clients have experienced a return on investment that makes their fees seem almost irrelevant.

For example, one of their clients—Fairfield, New Jersey–based MB Productions—is a video staging and production services company that has worked large events from the Tony Awards to concerts at Madison Square Garden. Kopp worked with the company to develop its message as well, and refine its target list of potential customers. To date, Kopp Consulting has secured 60 meetings because of its success in sharpening MB's target and messaging. The aggregate result is that MB Productions has already enjoyed $250,000 in new revenue—with double that in the pipeline from new and recurring business. And Kopp Consulting is only working for MB Productions for five hours per week!

By focusing on MB's benefits with precision and targeting the right prospective buyers, Kopp Consulting has opened doors to hundreds of thousands of sales. Currently, MB Production's return on investment is more than 14 times what they have spent with Kopp Consulting.

---

### Conduct a Message Strategy Session

Before you do any marketing, conduct your own message strategy session with your team:

1. What is the challenge our product or service overcomes?
2. What are the words our customers are using to describe their challenges?
3. What is our solution (using words they will relate to)?
4. What are the specific benefits of our product or service?
5. List your benefits with clear messaging for each targeted prospect.

## What Do Customers Really Want?

Sometimes what clients want doesn't even exist yet.

Juice company Odwalla was founded in Santa Cruz, California, in 1980 by Greg Steltenpohl, Gerry Percy, and Bonnie Bassett. The trio took the idea of selling fruit juices from a business guidebook, and they began by squeezing orange juice with a secondhand juicer in a shed in Steltenpohl's backyard. Their plan was to make enough profit to help fund music programs in local schools. They only had one box of oranges that first day, which they juiced with a $200 secondhand juicer, and delivered it to restaurants around town. The profits from that first day allowed them to buy two boxes of oranges to juice for day two of their business They used slogans for their product like "Soil to Soul," "People to Planet," and "Nourishing the Body Whole."

The name for their start-up, "Odwalla," was taken from a character who guided "the people of the sun" out of the "gray haze" in one of the founders' favorite song-poems, "Illistrum." Steltenpohl, Percy, and Bassett related this to their products, which they believed "help humans break free from the dull mass of over-processed foods so prevalent today." They truly wanted to create an antidote to fast food, and basically use it to change the world.

Odwalla was driven by a corporate conscience and goal of leading the public toward a closer-to-nature way of nourishing their bodies. The juices were highly rated for taste. But the true success came in the way that the company appealed to its customers.

The company decided not to follow the prewritten formulas for marketing and sales. Instead, the founders hired marketing and advertising experts, and created what they called their "Drink Tank"—a group responsible for developing and managing the Odwalla brand. In building the brand, members of the Drink Tank focused on authenticity, alignment, clear narrative, and the value of a strong corporate culture.

With little advertising, Odwalla differentiated its brand by extolling the benefits of drinking and supporting a "juice with a conscience." People cared and followed and bought. Odwalla spread the Soil to Soul slogan and its other messages primarily through its own direct to store delivery system.

"We created huge, very lively moving billboards out of the trucks," said David Bernard, an original member of the Odwalla Drink Tank. "And the drivers had really great 'Odwallawear' . . . fun, colorful shirts with great slogans, bright colors, and design. Everybody wanted an Odwalla shirt."

"There was also the 'Odwallazone.' To avoid having to pay slotting fees to larger grocery store chains, the sales team pioneered a strategy whereby they provided and maintained a cooler in exchange for space; primarily end aisle, and often in the produce department. Odwallazone had a cooler design and messaging that just could not be ignored; so stores loved them. They looked fantastic, and they sold a lot of juice."

The product's message and benefits spread widely enough to bring Odwalla into the mainstream. Ultimately, Odwalla focused on being meaningful to people—an advantage that went far beyond the drink's great taste.

After the Odwalla brand was sold to Coke, Odwalla Drink Tank alumni Don Faia, David Bernard, Tom Dill, and Bonno Bernard formed their own Santa Cruz, California–based advertising firm called Mythmaker where they apply the lessons and philosophies gained while at Odwalla.

"The big buzz word in marketing today is 'sustainable brands.' There's even a whole conference dedicated to the subject now," said David Bernard, Mythmaker's director of creative services. "We pioneered a lot of these ideas at Odwalla back in the late 1980s and early 1990s by actively positioning products with causes or a larger vision. We have been able to successfully communicate lofty ideals in fun and often irreverent ways."

## Do You Have a Strong Call to Action for Buyers?

Let's say that you have your valuable product or service, and have established compelling benefits and messaging to prospects. But have you asked anyone to specifically *do* something?

A call to action (CTA) is a critical concept in marketing; without it, you may miss out on many sales.

It's a single, focused command to your prospect. You constantly see different calls to action—statements like, Buy Now, Click Here, Call Today, Find Out More, Use this Coupon before December 31. Marketers have tested the effects of CTAs over and over again, and have found that they really do lead people to act. So tell your customers what you'd like them to do.

The first thing to remember is to keep it simple. Don't have 10 steps to your request. Provide a single, easy action for your customers to take (for example "Click Here!"). Realize, however, that your call to action may not lead them to buy immediately; there may need to be several before they make a purchase. It could be that the first call to action is to download a free report you wrote on a valuable topic (first CTA: download a free report). The next step may be to sign up for your e-mail newsletter (second CTA: sign up now). The final step may be to buy a product you are promoting in your newsletter (third CTA: Click Here to Buy Now).

List your most effective calls to action (and future ones you can think of).

_____

_____

_____

_____

## The Specifics of a Call to Action

Principle-Centered Marketing coach Jim Ackerman of Salt Lake City, Utah, has helped literally thousands of businesses of all sizes achieve remarkable growth in short periods of time. Ackerman said that it is about "cultivating desire" in the company's call to action. And he is so confident that this type of marketing works that he *guarantees* a 400 percent return on investment to clients—or they get their money back.

So what does Ackerman know that is so unique that he can make such a guarantee? "It is all about making a compelling offer," Ackerman stated. "Marketing should not just be about feeling good. People demand results today. Brand building has now taken a back seat to sales."

One of Ackerman's clients—a small retail card store—was looking to boost sales. They had a lot of overstocked merchandise that they needed to sell to make room for newer products. Ackerman created a personal letter for the owner to send to his best customers informing them of a "private sale" on Hallmark collectibles and other items in the store. The sale was held after regular store hours, and no one was admitted without the letter. The call to action here was to come to the private sale for significant discounts and exclusive access. And the fact that it really was "private" was a strong motivator for people who collect these types of items. The customers flocked to the store, and purchased $19,000 in overstocked items. One letter, one offer—and $19,000 in sales that would not have otherwise been made.

### Take 15 and Get Your Clients Going Wild!
#### A 15-Minute Client-Builder Exercise

List your product's or service's best benefit, compelling message, and call to action to buy.

_____

_____

_____

_____

# Third Principle
# Go Viral!

## Create Memorable Impactful Messaging Worthy of a Pass-Along

*Most good word of mouth is not generated through the Internet—it is passed along by people.*

V iral marketing" is the term for the phenomenon where individuals pass along a marketing message to others, thereby causing exponential growth in the message's exposure and impact. It is incredibly powerful, and has proven to far outperform the impact and results experienced from other marketing methods. At its core, viral marketing is about the rapid spread of a certain way of thinking about a product or service, and how it affects those interested.

### Marketing versus Viral Marketing

A typical marketing message or advertisement attempts to interrupt people to get their attention, but the act of interrupting is actually an inefficient approach to marketing. A better strategy is to have an attractive message that has been introduced by someone to whom the target is already paying attention, and whom that person trusts. With the increased availability of technology, a message can spread virally faster than ever. And the most powerful benefit of this kind of marketing is that others are doing some of your most important (and expensive) work *for* you!

## It Spreads Like a Contagious Virus

A viral message is one that moves and builds and "infects" everyone it touches. The message itself provokes people to spread the word. Like a cold or other kinds of viruses that make us sick, viral marketing takes advantage of rapid multiplication to carry a message quickly to a large population. But viral marketing has a far more positive effect than the common cold; in fact, it can be the most authentic and successful marketing strategy in a business's arsenal.

Recently, the H1N1 strain of influenza virus ("swine flu") sparked fear because of the health dangers it presents and the speed at which it travels from person to person. The spread of a virus is influenced by several recognized factors that must be present for a virus to become an epidemic.

*Four Contagion Factors of a Virus*

1. *Strength* of the virus

2. *Size* of the population of opportunity

3. *Number of days* contagious

4. *Number of people* a carrier comes in contact with

## An Idea Virus

The goal of many marketers today is to create an idea that has the properties listed above. Sometimes it happens by accident, and sometimes by design. Whether it's intended or not, this movement is called an "idea virus." It is an idea notion or practice that's transmitted from person to person through speech, gestures, the Internet, e-mail, or other media. It ignites and motivates people to move the message.

Seth Godin contends in his book, *Unleashing the Ideavirus* (Hyperion, 2001) that a commercial during the Super Bowl is a risky bet; a flashy web site is almost certain to lead to failure; and while hiring a celebrity spokesperson *might* work, it likely won't break through the clutter. Godin claims that, "Whenever advertisers build their business around the strategy of talking directly to the customer, they become slaves to the math of interruption marketing." Godin's book itself was an *idea virus*, and one that he released for free in a PDF format so that people could read it, learn from it, and e-mail it to each other. It quickly became one of the most downloaded e-books of all time, and it's still available—at no cost—at www.ideavirus.com.

## Give Away Valuable Products or Services

"Free" is the most powerful word in a marketer's vocabulary. Most viral marketing programs give away valuable products or services to attract attention—free benefits, information, software programs, or downloads. But you have to be prepared for delayed gratification. Though you may not see results immediately, if your campaign generates interest, profit is not far away. "Free" almost always attracts new contacts, names, e-mail addresses, interests, and general information. It is a simple formula: If you give something away, you will eventually have more people to whom you can sell.

It's essential that you do everything possible to make it easier for people to access information or material that may go viral, which means that you must allow people to:

- Download the content in easily viewable format (PDF, jpeg, mpeg).
- Embed the content into their own sites.
- Send it to friends, either by using a link or sending the content directly.
- Allow clients to send the message easily through social media sites like Twitter, Facebook, or others by simply clicking a button taking them to that site.

### Giving It Away

My company, Red Zone Marketing, has spent time creating a variety of tools, workbooks, books, and guides that were designed for professionals in order to help them plan their marketing and establish a business strategy. However, we recently considered the fact that the people who could benefit from these tools might never know about them and their value. So we decided to give some of it away (*What, are you kidding me!*), and now offer free downloads of previously sold products. One of these is the Red Zone Business Planning Template. It is a 20-page guide to planning your business and marketing. Lo and behold—within one day of announcing this free offer, we had *hundreds* of downloads from people we did not know; *thousands* in weeks; and who knows how many over time.

There were some people who thought we were crazy for giving away something that could be sold for cold hard cash—and told us so. But that's where the truth lies. Could we really sell thousands or hundreds of thousands of our products without doing something like that? Could we reach this many people in such a short amount of time—and for free—to let them know about everything we offer? And perhaps the biggest question: Where is the *real* money going to be made? On a $49.99 tool? Or through the process of building trust and confidence in thousands that may become followers, tell others about our firm, and eventually become loyal buyers of other products and clients for life?

We decided to take the chance and give up the $49.99, and so far, it has proved incredibly valuable. One result of this took place when my book, *The Connectors: How the World's Most Successful Businesspeople Build Relationships and Win Clients for Life* (John Wiley & Sons, Inc., 2009) was released; we had access to thousands of people who were already familiar with some of our materials that they received for free or purchased. The book immediately began selling fast both in bookstores and through online booksellers immediately on publication. We had already built some level of trust with potential readers, and were able to capitalize on the viral travel of some of our free products to sell the newest tool we had available. (Hopefully, this book you are reading now is the result of another generation of valuable content spreading!)

This truly is an effective way of marketing and selling—proving your worth, earning followers, and continuing to provide value that people come back for again and again.

> Consider something that may be an "idea virus" in your business. List potential ideas that have the power to spread from one person to another.
>
> _____
> _____
> _____
> _____

## Invoke Feelings!

The most important element of a viral campaign is to elicit strong emotions in prospective clients. You want people to feel one or more of the following:

- Hope
- Love

- Happiness
- Excitement
- Hate
- Anger

Your viral marketing campaign may well incite a strong emotional reaction from some people who love it, and some who do not. That's what happens with messages that provoke intense reactions.

For example, the Australian government promoted what it described simply as "the best job in the world" with a creative and extremely successful Internet campaign. The position they were advertising was a six-month contract to be caretaker of a series of islands in the Great Barrier Reef (off Australia's coast). The pay was $100,000, and the person selected for the position will broadcast weekly video blogs that promote the area. The government released the story through traditional media (Reuters) and then sustained the buzz over an array of online networks, including YouTube, Ning, Twitter, and Facebook. The contest's web site received one million hits the day after its launch, when the campaign's goal had been to receive just 400,000 hits over the course of the year. Furthermore, the program attracted more than 34,000 applicants, and generated more than $70 million worth of global publicity.

## A Simple, Repeatable Message

A simple marketing message is transmitted easily, and without degradation of the meaning and content. A short, clear message is best. For instance, Google, for the most part, does not and certainly did not advertise its initial offering of the web search site www.google.com. Think about how you found out about this search engine. People were passing along the straightforward message that you can, "Search for anything and everything on the Internet for free at www.google.com." The message became viral and the company's growth notoriously exploded. It's a truly a great example of a simple, repeatable statement of value.

## Exploit Common Wants, Needs, and Motivations

Greed, popularity, weight loss, comedy, and the desire to be loved are all examples of human motivators. Successful viral marketing frequently takes advantage of these or other common triggers. The message takes hold and spreads quickly if people feel an urge to share it with others. The key is to design a marketing strategy that builds on common motivations and behaviors to encourage its rapid transmission. An example of such powerful exploitation is the Atkins Diet phenomenon. It seemed that out of nowhere, millions of people had taken carbohydrates out of their diets, began eating meat and fat more frequently—and were somehow managing to lose weight. Word like this spreads quickly and widely.

## Watershed Moments for a Viral Message

In November 2007, public relations veteran and president of Ericho Communications Eric Yaverbaum, along with advertising veteran and founding partner of DiMassimo Goldstein Mark DiMassimo (DIGO), created *Tappening*, a campaign and web site (www.tappening.com) designed to educate the public about the massive and unnecessary waste of fossil fuels and resultant stress on the environment caused by the bottled water industry. The movement was meant to encourage people to drink tap water whenever possible. A little over a year after the launch of this "campaign to make tap water cool," bottled water sales declined in the United States, and Tappening has, almost accidentally, become a profitable business venture.

Tappening's highly chronicled and trafficked web site has received almost 8.5 million page views to date, and features thousands of articles on the bottled water versus tap water debate, as well as a National Tap Water Quality Database. "We believed we could use our advertising and public relations abilities to un-sell bottled water hype," DiMassimo explained. "We aimed to create the kind of brand that bottled water has for tap water."

Yaverbaum and DiMassimo each invested personally in the start-up; so in an effort to sustain and self-fund the campaign, the partners decided to sell well-designed, reusable water bottles on their educational web site. Each bottle says either "Think Global, Drink Local" or "What's Tappening?" The pair thought their initial inventory would carry them through their first year. To their surprise, the bottles became immediately trendy, and the entire first stock—all 39,000 bottles—sold out within 36 hours of the site going live. "It was a viral reaction. I've learned very quickly, firsthand, the potential power of viral marketing," said Yaverbaum.

Soon, Yaverbaum's publicity machinery kicked into gear. National television appearances and coast-to-coast radio interviews ensued, and newspaper articles and bloggers alike touted both the information from the Tappening web site and the bottles themselves. Schools and universities called; Yaverbaum and DiMassimo would have needed their own jet to show up everywhere they'd been invited for Earth Day. *Good Morning America* featured the Tappening bottle on their New Year's Day program, citing it as one of the "hottest products for 2008." *Adweek* magazine touted Tappening as "a form of business philanthropy . . . founded to right a perceived wrong." *People* magazine photographed the bottles for its pages, and "Tappening" soon became part of the vernacular. *Business Week* twice referred to the trend's popularity by reporting that, "Marriott hotels have joined the tappening movement."

Tappening's product line soon grew to include stainless steel bottles as well as BPA-free plastic ones, and a duffle-type bag created out of 100 percent post-consumer recyclables (single-serve water bottles and yogurt containers). The most recent offering in the Tappening web site store—for people who are seriously concerned about the quality of their tap water— is e-WaterTest (www.e-watertest.com), which offers professional lab testing for 150 possible contaminants.

Tappening's unanticipated business success has been gratifying, but Yaverbaum and DiMassimo's greatest satisfaction has come from the public's responsiveness to their cause, the role they're playing in helping to make tap the water of choice, and in weaning people off single-serve disposables. On September 10, 2008, a Senate subcommittee held a hearing on the quality and environmental issues surrounding bottled water, and sales have been steadily declining.

Yaverbaum concludes by stating that, "It's my hope that Tappening can serve as one kind of business model for others who would like to promote a cause or issue that's meaningful, and serves what they deem to be a higher good while also allowing them to thrive economically." This is a solid example of a business that has managed to evoke a highly emotional reaction in its followers.

## Be Exciting or They Will Never Be Interested

People will talk and spread the word about you if there is anything worth saying—good *or* bad. The more intensely they feel about your company or message, the more they will talk. But in order to get people to talk, you must earn it.

If your message is not exciting or enticing, you will have to spend more time, effort, and money than humanly possible to elicit people's interest. For example: A film titled *The Blair Witch Project* was released on July 14, 1999. It cost about $350,000 to produce and went on to gross nearly $250 million—giving it the highest profit-to-cost ratio of any film in history. This low-budget film's unprecedented success could be attributed to the unique web site the filmmakers designed that told what seemed to be a true story unfolding. Everyone wondered—was it fact or fiction? The site spoke convincingly of the mythology behind the infamous Blair Witch; displayed a realistic photo of the three filmmakers accompanied by a caption claiming that it had been taken "less than a week before their disappearance"; and included a sideshow of other rather generic yet seemingly authentic photos that made many believe that this site was truly legitimate. This got people talking and passing the message along, and created an insatiable interest in the movie.

## Give Clients More Than They Expect

If you want people to notice your campaign, you may have to do something that your clients don't expect. Forget about trying to promote your products as "great," or attempt to make your materials look impressive; everyone else has already done that. In fact, you may want to forget about you, your product, or your company, and instead focus exclusively on creating a good and interesting story.

In 2006, a relatively unknown online guitar lesson service called Guitar MasterPro.net became an international sensation when they released a basic, nonprofessionally produced, uncreative video of one its students sitting in his room playing an electric guitar version of "Pachelbel's Canon." The 21-year-old's talent prompted an international video-sharing bonanza that has resulted in more than 60 million views on YouTube, making it one of the site's most-viewed submissions. The young guitarist said simply in his description box on YouTube, "I learned to play guitar with Guitar MasterPro.net." Now *that's* proof!

## Get Affiliates to Spread the Word

Implement a coordinated effort to get other outlets to spread your message. Turn it into an article and/or press release and distribute it to bloggers, web sites, and the media. When you give away free articles that include valuable information, others may well post this material on their web sites. Hundreds of media outlets can pick up a press release and redistribute the subject matter to thousands of potential readers. Now someone *else* is delivering your message, as well as providing an implied endorsement for your company and/or product.

List possible affiliates that would be interested in your message.

_____

_____

_____

_____

## Creating a Network

Most people have 15 to 20 people in their close group of friends, family, and associates, while his or her broader network may consist of hundreds or thousands of people. For example, a bank teller or waitress may communicate regularly with hundreds of customers in a given week. Network marketers have long understood the power of both kinds of these human connections; the strong, close bonds as well as the broader networked relationships. Social networking on the Internet helps to develop this kind of a system of associations that will rapidly move a powerful message (see Chapter 13, "Social Media").

## Learning from Ponzi and Pyramid Schemes

Ponzi schemes and related investment pyramid schemes can actually serve as early examples of viral marketing. Basically, participants or investors are paid interest from the principal deposits of those who invest later on. These plans have been successful because enthusiastic participants recruit their friends who then recruit *their* friends—resulting in exponential growth. The arrangement collapses when the participants have tapped out on their recruiting or when—in the case of Bernie Madoff—the market collapses.

Multilevel marketing is similar but an ethical form of viral marketing. It was popularized in the 1960s and 1970s so that representatives could gain income by marketing products among their circles of influence, and give their friends a chance to similarly market products. Examples include Amway, Shaklee, and Mary Kay Cosmetics, among many others. When successful, the strategy creates an exponentially growing network of representatives and greatly enriches adopters.

## Create Your Own Marketing "Epidemic"

This approach requires that you follow several contagion factors to get—and keep—your message moving. Using the medical contagion factors for the spread of a virus listed previously; here are the four marketing factors for spreading a message virally.

*The Four Contagion Factors of Viral Marketing*
1. *Strength of the message*. The message or offering has to be worthy, interesting, and valuable in order for it to grab people's attention and begin to spread.

2. *Size of the population of opportunity.* The number of potential people with whom the message will connect must be significant. It has to truly resonate with a defined segment(s) of the population.

3. *Number of days contagious.* Moving the message forward is critical to keeping it alive and mobile. The more you can release valuable information over time, the longer the contagious period's length will be.

4. *Number of people message carriers have in their network.* The message needs to touch as many points of contact as possible—clients, alliances, prospects, bloggers, media, and friends. If these people feel compelled to share with their entire network of people, and their networks are large enough, the message can go viral.

---

## Does Your Idea Meet the Four Contagion Factors?

1. Strength of the message.
2. Size of the population of opportunity.
3. Potential number of days the message will be contagious.
4. Number of people message carriers have in their network.

---

## Take 15 and Get Your Clients Going Wild!
### A 15-Minute Client-Builder Exercise

Consider what kind of viral campaigns you and your company can create. List the idea, message, and the details on how it could be distributed, such as specific people who can spread the message and forums for getting the word out.

_____

_____

_____

_____

## CHAPTER 5

# Fourth Principle Leverage Your Business Network for Incremental Growth

## Find and Cultivate Centers of Influence to Move Your Message Fast

I f you have a great idea, product, or service and no one knows about it, does it really exist? Technically, yes; but it's a bit like the oft-asked philosophy question, "If a tree falls in a forest and there's no one there to hear it, does it make a sound?" The obvious answer is, "Of course!" But for years, philosophers have claimed that sound is only sound if a person hears it; and the same could be said for your product or service. If you've designed something for other people who simply don't use it or know about it, in philosophers' eyes, it really doesn't exist. If you have something extraordinary, but no one buys it, then it may as well not even have been created. You must attract people to your product or service and get them to latch on to the idea.

## Sales 101 versus Advanced Sales Strategies

The most skilled salespeople build strong business relationships. They may start at a cold call, follow it with a series of contacts, face-to-face meetings, and presentations, and use these to turn the prospect into a paying client. However, this Sales 101 process is doubtlessly the most difficult way to grow new account sales, even—and especially—for the most experienced salesperson. Yet this is how the system of sales is being taught—that salespeople need to execute a plan designed to reach out systematically, one-on-one, with potential buyers.

Whether you enjoy enormous results using this process or have only limited successes, at some point in time, the drive to make an endless amount of calls and contacts weakens. Sales 101 strategies are the primary method you will use to garner new business when you are new to sales and don't have any clients or customers to speak of. When you start becoming successful, however, the desire to continuously undergo this process diminishes. Yet a salesperson charged with bringing on new sales must somehow continue to open new doors.

Thankfully for salespeople everywhere, there *are* new and profitable strategies for leveraging themselves. It requires a plan, but influencing current relationships can be the miracle answer to the typical grind of prospecting. *Advocates, centers of influence, and your customers will give you referrals and introductions that are critical to expanding your reach and incremental sales growth.* But who wants to connect you with others? Lots of people do! You just need to find out—and show them—what's in it for them.

## Finding True Centers of Influence

A productive business network is filled with well-connected, influential people who share your target market. These individuals are often called Centers of Influence; they are usually associated with and respected by others important to you and your business, and have a complementary rather than a competing service or product. A legitimate center of influence is in the habit of connecting people, whereas a regular business associate does not normally do so, and therefore needs and expects different things from you.

To effectively leverage a business network, it is critical to have businesspeople who are actively marketing and have a relationship with you within your network. Many professionals make the mistake of attempting to utilize a business network that is too small to produce ample activity.

## Build Your Connections—Even Introverts Can Do It!

You might not be the type of person who loves to socialize, attend big parties, and network whenever you get the chance. If so—that's okay! One of the more surprising things I discovered when interviewing success-ful businesspeople for my first book, *The Connectors* (John Wiley & Sons, Inc., 2009), was that those who were masters at leveraging their business relationships did not focus on creating relationships with *everyone*. But they *did* have a plan for reaching those with whom they wanted to mean-ingfully connect. It doesn't matter whether you are introverted or extro-verted; what matters is that you've spent some time thinking about which relationships are most vital and why.

In fact, someone who is most likely the nation's best-known network-ing professional recently realized that he is an introvert. Ivan Misner, PhD—founder of BNI, the world's largest networking organization, and author of 11 books on networking—shared this newfound discovery with me. *What?* Misner told me that his wife of 20 years informed him during dinner one night that he displayed many introvert tendencies. Needless to say, Misner was shocked; after all, he wondered, how could a professional speaker and the founder of the largest networking organization be an in-trovert? His wife's observation prompted him to take an online personality assessment test—the results of which revealed that he was a "situational extrovert," or was reserved around strangers but outgoing in the right con-text. Misner explained, "It struck me that I started BNI [because] I was naturally uncomfortable meeting new people. BNI created a system that enabled me to meet people in an organized, structured, networking envi-ronment that did not require that I actually . . . talk to strangers."

---

### The Connector Plan: Where Do I Start?

In order to form potential influential relationships, it's best to begin by determining where and with whom your most important rela-tionships already do—and could—exist. Ask yourself: With whom do I need to be able to connect to build my business successes? List your potential Powerful Connections List:

*(continued)*

(*continued*)

*Powerful Connections List*

1. _____

2. _____

3. _____

4. _____

5. _____

6. _____

7. _____

8. _____

9. _____

10. _____

11. _____

12. _____

13. _____

14. _____

15. _____

16. _____

17. _____
    _____

18. _____
    _____

19. _____
    _____

20. _____
    _____

Continue this list to 100 people. In addition, choose the top 20 people on your list with whom you have—or want to have—a strong relationship. Make a point of meeting with them every six weeks to strengthen your connections. Leverage your business associations effectively by creating a large enough network, staying in touch with them regularly, helping them get to know you, what you do in your business, and the kinds of people with whom you work. But most of all, concentrate on getting to know *them*, and developing a relationship focused on their needs.

## Partnering with Future Advocates on a Limited Budget

With little to no money to back your new, interesting, and beneficial product or service, what do you do? Innovative thinkers figure out a way to get the message to the masses without spending much. In fact, even if you have a large marketing budget, it is sometimes better to first consider what you might do if you didn't. This forces you to look at paths that actually bring better results for some businesses than spending enormous sums of money with traditional marketing does.

For example—Shea Megale is 14-year-old author of a successful book series called *Marvelous Mercer*, but she is no ordinary girl. Shea has spinal muscular atrophy, a paralyzing disease that has left her with limited arm strength and compromised motor skills. To help her get around more independently, Shea has a companion dog named Mercer. Mercer knows 60 commands that include turning on lights and opening doors.

Shea's first book began as several entries in her diary that her mother Megan discovered. They were sketches and stories of Mercer the dog ice-skating and doing other activities, all depicted in great detail by a little girl who never would be able to do enjoy any of these activities. However, she was experiencing them through her dog—and her imagination. Her mother was so moved by the incredible stories and the meaning behind them that she vowed to get Shea's works published.

But getting a book to market and then publicizing it is no easy task, especially with no extra money to support this venture. While the Megales managed to find a family member to illustrate the book, they realized that promoting it would be the key to success. Friends told Megan that USA Today should run a story on Shea and her book; but getting through to the right person at the right time can be extremely difficult at large media outlets. The key is getting the media to pay attention. So Megan did some research, and found out that the editor was originally from New York.

"We lived 5 miles from the USA Today headquarters," Megan said. "Knowing that New Yorkers in the Washington DC area sometimes miss Carvel ice cream, I drove to Carvel, bought some ice cream and had them write on the top 'PLEASE CALL ME.' I drove the ice cream to the gate and delivered it as if I was a courier. I knew they would have to deliver it immediately to the editor to whom it was addressed; otherwise it would melt. The editor called me 10 minutes later." The following Saturday Shea and her book were featured in a two-page spread in USA Today.

Megan has used other unique approaches to get her daughter's book into famed Manhattan toy store FAO Schwartz, and partnered with Build-A-Bear workshop stores. Instead of taking normal channels, Megan walked directly into the FAO office in New York and left with a deal. She also wrote a letter to Build-A-Bear founder and chief executive Maxine Clark after reading Clark's book. Clark responded, and shortly afterward, they had worked out the details for a partnership.

Reaching out personally has been the key to Megan's ability to form the partnerships necessary to get the word out about Shea's books. No matter how great the books are and how impactful Shea's story is, no one knows about any of it until Megan and Shea form partnerships with powerful allies. Shea is currently writing her fourth book in a six-book series. Proceeds from all the books help support spinal muscular atrophy research and Canine Companions for Independence, a nonprofit organization that provides highly trained assistance dogs for children and adults with disabilities free of charge. Book sales have contributed more than $600,000 to these charities.

Consider the methods that Megan Megale used to get in touch with the people she knew would support her daughter's remarkable project. What are some innovative ways you can target and reach your potential advocates?

_____

_____

_____

_____

## Strategic Partnerships

Brian F. O'Connell, director of strategic partnership at Interdev (Seattle, Washington) was quoted in 1998 saying, "In the business world, radically changing socioeconomic realities, along with the demand for a higher return on investment, led to the acknowledgment long ago that . . . strategic alliances and partnerships have now turned former competitors into new collaborators."

A *strategic alliance* takes place when two separate businesses work together to offer a broader set of skills or services to joint clients, thereby providing a mutual benefit to all involved parties. This kind of partnership allows both companies to create an advantage over competitors by broadening the scope of their operations. The respective sizes of the partnering firms are of little consequence. What is essential for the alliance to be successful is that it must benefit both partners, and be rooted in mutual trust and respect.

Developing and leveraging strategic alliances can be used to great advantage in almost any profession. A financial advisor can team with an accountant; a real estate agent can connect with a moving company; or a personal trainer can form a relationship with a nutritional supplement store. In today's competitive world, the strategic alliance can be a fantastic Red Zone Marketing tool. By "joining forces" informally or formally with a partner, you can greatly increase your chances for success; and ultimately, realize greater profits.

Whatever your company's shortcomings, they can be overcome by teaming up with someone who exhibits considerable strength in that area. There are two basic types of alliances—similar industry and separate industry. Both have the potential to provide you with a stream of referrals and new business—without a large marketing budget.

## Similar Industry Alliances

The concepts of one-stop shopping and full-service offerings are becoming increasingly popular among consumers. Creating these kinds of conveniences for your clients through strategic alliances can distinguish you from your competition, and make it easy for clients to buy from you.

For example, sports agents—who are often lawyers—represent athletes (clients) in contract negotiations with prospective teams. Many new situations and opportunities arise once the athlete has signed a contract. Newly acquired riches need to be properly managed, and there's also the potential for landing marketing contracts with businesses (for example: shoe, automobile, and soft-drink companies). Both of these are important second steps for the newly signed athlete and present the agent with further opportunities to serve his client by teaming up with a financial advisor and a marketing specialist who can provide advice and guidance in what is new and unfamiliar territory for the athlete.

Other potential alliances might include weight trainers, accountants, and real estate companies. The strategic partners may pay a referral fee to the agent, or the agent may share in the profits. Or the agent may choose to simply base this connection on a give-and-take referral relationship with no money changing hands. The agent could acquire new clients based on the recommendation of a strategic alliance partner and vice versa. With the proper alliances in place, all parties will reap the benefits.

## Separate Industry Alliances

This type of an alliance is not set up for one-stop shopping, but instead leverages the fact that two or more separate businesses have the same target market. It requires that you establish a system in which partners arrange to consistently and systematically supply each other with referrals and information. For example, a dry-cleaning business could partner with the upscale grocery store located next door. The dry cleaner knows that the grocery shoppers are the same types of customers who regularly have their clothing dry cleaned, so he approaches the grocery store manager with a plan for a strategic marketing alliance. The dry cleaner provides coupons to be handed out at the checkout of the grocery store, offering a 10 percent discount on dry-cleaning services. In return, the dry cleaner staples coupons to the plastic dry-cleaning bag that offer a grocery store product—perhaps a free gallon of milk or a gourmet salad—to customers who spend a specified amount for dry cleaning.

Consider the types of customers and clients you have, and the other products or services they regularly use, as well as your business's location(s). With what specific businesses might you create alliances?

1. _____
   _____

2. _____
   _____

3. _____
   _____

4. _____
   _____

5. _____
   _____

6. _____
   _____

7. _____
   _____

Informally or formally "joining forces" with a partner greatly increases your chances for success and, ultimately, allows you to realize greater profits. Whatever your shortcomings, they can be overcome by teaming up with someone who's strong in that area.

## Avoid the "Lone Ranger" Syndrome

There's an old African proverb that says, "If you want to go fast, go alone; if you want to go far, go together." If you haven't explored the possibility of forming strategic alliances with other companies, you may be missing an opportunity for greater growth and profitability than you can realize on your own.

## The Power of a "Harvard" Network

One of the reasons that people who have graduated from the nation's most prestigious colleges and universities become successful is because they are intelligent. This is, of course, the way in which they gained entrance into a top school in the first place, as projected with excellent grades and high SAT and ACT scores. But there is another real—yet not as frequently talked about—factor in their success: who they met along the way. People who attend Ivy League universities like Harvard and Princeton look out for each other; they connect with each other, hire each other, and refer to each other. The same can be said for many of the nation's higher-status schools. It may even be true that the alumni network is more valuable and important to graduates' successes than the education they received.

Now, if you're feeling particularly negative, you can think about how networks may also be responsible for underhanded activities. Actually, the power of the network is the reason it works and has worked since the beginning of time. It can, for example, be responsible for convicting people of insider trading and politicians giving jobs to their friends instead of going through fair and open proposal procedures (I live in Illinois, so I'm very aware of how this has worked for years). The privilege of the network is potent.

So what do you do if you *didn't* attend a prestigious college? The principles are the same for any network of people: those with similar interests, backgrounds, commonality, and relationships will look out for each other, work with each other, and help each other. It is human nature. So, if you don't already have a network, find one! Join a community, alumni, or industry group, and get involved. Create advocates and make yourself a known entity in the group through your activism.

---

Consider some groups you could join to build your own powerful network:

Charity _____

_____

Church Group _____

_____

Industry Group _____

_____

Alumni Group _____

_____

Rotary or other international organization _____

EO or other international entrepreneur organization with qualified entry standards _____

_____

---

# Against All Odds

Stephanie and Justin Bigart started off with no money, limited connections, and a dream of starting a spa. Sounds like most start-up small businesses, right? But today their company—Sage Spa Living, founded in October 2003 in Bozeman, Montana—has become a quick-start successful business with locations across the entire state. The Bigarts manufacture their own product lines, own the online store www.Sageborn.com, employ nearly 100 spa and salon professionals, and have donated thousands of dollars and countless hours to community organizations. Theirs is a real-life rags-to-riches success story.

When Stephanie and Justin began their venture in 2003, they were in their twenties. They had less than $1,000. To launch the business, the Bigarts knew they would need a great natural environment, high-quality product offerings, and superior customer service. But with almost no start-up capital, they were already fighting strong odds. Less than $1,000 doesn't go far when you need to design, furnish, stock, and staff the kind of spa the Bigarts imagined. And even if they could have financed 95 percent or more of their capital expenditures, the spa wouldn't have been able to generate enough cash flow to meet its interest and principal payments. The conventional approach would have been to settle for whatever they could afford at the time. But the Bigart's took a different approach—leveraging! And each relationship they leveraged has given them access to another one. Consider each of the following elements of their business:

*Location.* The Bigarts searched until they found a developer who was building new, high-end retail space in a historically underdeveloped block of Main Street. The developer was looking for high-quality retail tenants—which is exactly what Sage offered. In exchange, the developer gave them an unusually generous build-out allowance and a back-ended lease schedule. The Bigarts also engaged the services of a retail space designer in the area who wanted to enter the spa business. Sage got good design for not much money, and the designer walked away with a design statement for his portfolio.

*High-Quality Products.* The Bigarts learned that the product vendor with whom they wanted to work was looking to upgrade and consolidate its retail relationships. With its relatively large and now high-profile retail presence, Sage fit the bill. In exchange, the vendor offered an attractive employee training allowance and special inventory financing that allowed Sage to carry a complete product line, which, unlike its local competitors, Sage supports with dedicated staff.

*Prospective Service Providers/Employees.* Because of their attractive space and commitment to training, it didn't take the Bigarts long to find extraordinary employees. Sage was a unique business for Bozeman at the time—one that provided a different kind of experience and got people talking. As a consequence, the couple launched a differentiated company without spending any more than a conventional spa start-up would have cost. And Sage achieved breakeven revenue in its first week of operation and month-to-month revenue growth is in the double digits.[1]

---

### Four Steps to Leverage Your New Business Venture

Take a cue from the Bigart's business model, and consider the following four aspects of your company:

1. Write out your vision of exactly what you want and need to be successful quickly.
2. Identify people who can connect you to what you most want and need. Search and link to them as if you had no money—even if you do. A vision with no money needs great passion to survive.
3. Create a "What's In It for Them" plan to forge a leveraged relationship. List the reasons why each potential partner would want to work with you on your venture.
4. Begin reaching out in person, through the phone and via e-mail with your prepared plan to create win-win relationships. Get your business off the ground with little to no start-up capital if possible. The best capital is the connections you make.

---

## Bag Idea Creates Buying Frenzy

The quickest way to get your product to "exist" is to get it into the hands of "Connectors"—those people who would be willing to take what you have and connect it to others who may be interested. This is a form of leveraging, something that should be treated as a serious marketing strategy. The more leveraging you can do, the lower risk and higher potential for success.

For instance, veteran Realtor Jean Newell had an idea for her fellow real estate agents. She invented a personal utility pouch (PUP)—a multizippered minipack designed to carry all the technical tools, keys, contracts, and more that a real estate agent needs. Newell knew from the initial responses she received about the product that she was on to something that people wanted. Her next objective was to get on QVC, but she was turned down by gatekeepers again and again. So she decided to reach out to her network, which consisted of the people that she met and e-mailed in her years as a real estate agent—other agents, buyers, sellers, and so forth—and asked for their help. She sent out an e-mail requesting help to find a contact person at QVC for her new product, and received an overwhelming response. Within a few days, she had 40 e-mails from people providing contacts at QVC. "Some of the e-mails had been forwarded, forwarded, and forwarded to people far beyond my original network," Newell noted. Once she had the right contact names, she created a quick video to show how she would promote the bag and sent it off to QVC. Within two weeks she was accepted!

Since her initial appearance on QVC, Newell has become a sales superstar and media darling. She's been featured in countless newspapers, and has even enjoyed a recent appearance on NBC's *The Today Show*.

"Some people are afraid to ask for help," Newell said. "[But] I knew that people wouldn't find me, so I reached out to find them!"

## Mining Your Data for Relationships

A strategic challenge for many businesses today is coordinating the wealth of data that they have—specifically, the knowledge about relationships—to utilize it for marketing and business development.

The ability to mine your business relationship data is important because many service-based businesses generate significant revenue from existing connections and the strength of those relationships. Authors J. R. Harbison and P. Pekar Jr. conducted research on the performance of alliances, and determined:

- Strategic alliances have consistently produced a return on investment of nearly 17 percent among the top 2,000 companies in the world for nearly a decade. This return is 50 percent more than the average return on investment that the companies produced overall.
- The 25 companies most active in alliances achieved a 17.2 percent return on equity—40 percent more than the average return on equity of the Fortune 500.[2]

A tool that law and professional services firms often use to analyze and leverage their relationships is an Enterprise Relationship Management (ERM) system. ERM technology works to synergize the different types of relationships that a firm engages in in order to more effectively target business opportunities. This technology provides a "relationship search engine" that automatically maps the firm's entire external relationship network, uncovering connections to those outside the firm by calculating the strength of each association to an individual, company, or industry. The ERM software enables the firm to analyze e-mail traffic to determine who at the firm holds the strongest relationships with a specific person or company outside the firm. This type of data mining is often used for business development planning. After a list of potential new business opportunities are identified, those results can be run through the ERM system to automatically map who at the firm has the best chance of making an introduction.

The alternative for small businesses that would not purchase an ERM software system is to track through your current database. Code as much data as you can about each contact including company name, industry, number of employees, and so forth; then rank individuals as a "Connector Type" based on how connected they are within a network. Determine your own system based on A through D connectors. This allows you to instantly access this information and leverage your relationships for new business planning and acquisition efforts. Now that's valuable information to work with and plan around!

There is no doubt that when you take a hard look at what successful businesspeople do to grow incrementally, it is all about developing powerful relationships.

## Making a Career Out of Creating Alliances

An underrated area of expertise in business is the ability to create partnerships, especially as a formal job responsibility. But it is one of the most significant ways in which companies make profitable inroads with complementary product providers. Ben Sperling—current vice president, strategy and alliances at Awarepoint Corporation, a technology firm offering advanced technologies in the health-care industry—has spent his career forming alliances. He shares the following two factors, which he believes are vital in choosing a valuable strategic alliance partnership.

1. *Consider all possible partners*. Make a special consideration for the number two in the industry. Often, the terms are more positive and they may work harder for you.

2. *Fully research your potential partners*. Vet your potential partners through your networks (including LinkedIn) to find if someone else

has partnered with them and what successes they achieved and issues occurred.

Sperling also recommends designing and adhering to a formal process such as the following three points after your partnership has been formalized.

### Creating Profitable Alliances—Formal Process

1. *Create it.* Create a firm plan for going to market. Both sides must receive value, conduct specific activities, and commit certain resources. And the partnership should be about more than just financial reciprocation.
2. *Prioritize it.* Make sure that activities, as well as specific short- and long-term goals, are prioritized and agreed on.
3. *Assess the value.* Have formal, scheduled meetings to determine what both parties are gaining from the partnership, what's working and what isn't, and what needs to be changed.

## Delighted Clients Become Evangelists for You!

Don't ever forget that your clients are probably the best source of leveraging in your business, an advocacy often called referrals (see Chapter 11, "Your Best Prospects Come from Referrals"). When customers are truly delighted about their experience with your product or service, they can become outspoken promoters for your company. This group of satisfied believers can be your most powerful marketing force to gain sales and increase your exposure and influence, and can serve as an entire force of unofficial (and unpaid) salespeople. By deepening customer relationships, profitable organizations create communities that generate grassroots support and become leverage points for more business.

---

List ways in which your clients can serve as your advocates.

_____

_____

_____

_____

# Take 15 and Get Your Clients Going Wild!
## *A 15-Minute Client-Builder Exercise*

Record your leveraging strategy action items:

_____

_____

_____

_____

# Fifth Principle
# The Critical Importance
# of Execution in Your
# Game Plan

## Good Execution Is Better than Good Strategy

*The best marketing strategy is the one you can pull off completely.*

As a marketing consultant, I have found that business owners always want to find out which marketing strategies are producing results right now. This book is filled with information about strategies that have dramatic success, but there is an underlying factor that is often overlooked and rarely blamed for lack of success: execution.

Entrepreneurs have long attributed any success they experience to having a better product or service. But in today's fast-moving, completely networked world, superior execution is the clear force behind these accomplishments. Although small business owners are great at adopting many new marketing ideas, they're not always so good at finishing. Therefore, the best marketing strategy—whatever your company or industry—is the one you can pull off completely.

If a business chooses one particular approach—for instance, setting up a referral campaign—and carries out that one strategy until it's executed fully and with precision, it is implementing the best marketing strategy. It is not the strategy as much as its execution that achieves desirable results.

## What Are You Doing in *Your* Red Zone?

Poor execution is as significant an obstacle to business success as it is in just about everything in life, including military campaigns, transportation, manufacturing, and sports.

Let's take football, for example. If you're a football fan—and you don't have to be—you already know what the term *red zone* means. If you're not, here's a quick explanation: it's the final 20 yards through which a player must travel in order to score. It's that part of the playing field where the going is toughest; where the offensive team becomes acutely aware its objective is within range, and steps up its efforts accordingly. The team on defense digs in as well, knowing that their ability to deny their opponent the opportunity to score a touchdown or a field goal can spell the difference between victory and defeat.

I believe there is a similar area in business. I chose the term "Red Zone" for my marketing philosophy—and for the name of my company—for two reasons. First, the principles, strategies, and practices that winning football teams use in that area of the field are the same ones that allow successful businesses and professionals to grow and prosper. And second, my grandmother raised me to be a football fan and constantly emphasized the importance of those final 20 yards.

Before Vince Lombardi arrived in Green Bay in 1959, the team had not had a winning season since 1947, and the 1958 team had lost 10 of its 12 games. Lombardi immediately informed his players that he was used to winning, and he had no interest in being part of a losing team. In his first year, the team won seven games. By the time Lombardi stepped down after the 1967 season, the Packers had won five league championships in nine years, eight of their nine playoff games, and the first two Super Bowls.

Lombardi focused on the basics, and on getting results. Each year as the team gathered for the first time, he would stand at the front of the meeting room, hold up a football, and make this announcement: "Gentlemen, this is a football." His philosophy was simple, but effective: "Some people try to find things in this game or put things into it which don't exist. Football is two things. It's blocking and tackling. . . . You block and tackle better than the team you're playing, you win."

As a highly in-demand as a speaker, Lombardi would often tell his audiences: "Running a football team is no different than running any other kind of organization—an army, a political party, or a business. The principles are the same. The object is to win."

Let's consider how his words apply to the professional world. Winners in business are unconditionally committed to their goals, to accomplishing the results that consistently mean victory. Much like victorious football teams, every successful business and professional organization has a game plan—an essential ingredient of which is marketing. Every phase of your marketing plan should be designed to get you into the red zone, and then to score; in other words, to get the results you want.

And championship teams don't just make their way to the red zone more; once there, they execute to perfection and achieve their desired outcome. The confidence that transforms a losing team into a Super Bowl champion—and which can change *any* sales and marketing team into a top performing one—comes from developing the type of consistent red zone thinking that generates a game plan that every member of the team understands and supports. Winning is the direct result of confidence and preparation. It's not about "winging it," or drawing up plays on the spur of the moment; rather, it comes from executing your game plan with precision.

## When Do You Give Up?

Though execution is critical to success, strategy is certainly not unimportant. If you implement a poor method with perfection, you're not likely to achieve the outcome you want. The goal is to develop tactics to which you've given thought and consideration, based on the realistic possibilities for your business. You must then implement those tactics to completion. Unfortunately, many businesses give up too early on a particular approach when they don't see immediate results. They then begin the long process of employing another strategy, followed by another, and so on. The real problem here occurs when companies try to execute a game plan that is focused on implementing outdated or poorly considered strategies.

Do you know when you and your team members should give up on a strategy? It can be difficult, because there is a fine line between giving up too quickly and riding a dead horse. The key is to thoughtfully evaluate your plan based on its qualitative and quantitative results—not just one or the other.

> How much time and effort do you put into evaluating your marketing strategies?
>
> _____
>
> _____
>
> _____
>
> _____

## Riding Dead Horses

To give yourself the best chance at success, you may want to look at _what_ you're executing. Maybe you're using a game plan that worked in the past but that currently doesn't seem to be getting you into the red zone—or across the goal line—as often as it once did. Maybe it's because the same old strategies you've been using for years just don't work in today's fast-paced, high-tech, constantly changing world. Perhaps, as the centuries-old cliché goes, you've been "beating a dead horse." The results you're seeking haven't changed, but the strategies you're using are no longer effective.

According to legend, there's a bit of wisdom that the Dakota Indians—a branch of the Sioux—have passed down from generation to generation: "When you discover you're riding a dead horse, the best strategy is to dismount."

Good advice, indeed, but all too often ignored in today's business world, especially among those whose philosophy is, "But we've always done it this way." Some time ago, while browsing the Internet, I came across the following anonymous list of 10 "dead horse" strategies (or game plans) that many organizations adopt when they're not getting the results they want:

1. Buying a stronger whip.
2. Changing riders.
3. Threatening the horse with termination.
4. Appointing a committee to study the horse.
5. Arranging to visit other sites to see how _they_ ride dead horses.
6. Hiring outside contractors to ride the dead horse.

7. Harnessing several dead horses together for increased speed.

8. Donating the dead horse to a recognized charity, and deducting its full original cost.

9. Doing a time-management study to see if lighter riders would improve productivity.

10. Declaring a dead horse has lower overhead, and therefore performs better.

## A Better Game Plan

During the football season, coaches begin drawing up their plans for next week's game as soon as this week's game ends. They spend the week watching hours and hours of film of their own games and those of their opponents. They look for ways to improve their own performance and exploit the perceived weaknesses of the adversary. The goals never change, but based on the research they've done, they'll develop a strategy that they believe will give them the best chance to win.

Just imagine if small businesses spent this much time putting together their game plan for success—even just once during the year. Football teams do extensive strategy evaluation once a week during the season. And because they are working so hard at coming up with the best plan, the thing that varies from week to week is often not the strategy, but its execution. If they're playing in a game with a plan that originally called for running the football 75 percent of the time, but the first 10 or 15 running plays are stopped cold and the team still hasn't scored—the coaches will realize they've been "beating a dead horse." They'll quickly begin calling pass plays in order to win, hoping a different, well thought-out strategy, implemented well, will achieve the desired results.

If you've been riding a dead horse, take the Dakotas' advice: dismount! Your goals don't have to change, but you need to try to reach them in a different way. You don't want 50 different strategies, each implemented partially; you must operate according to a single, fully considered and developed plan.

## Adjusting Your Course

Les Taylor is a professional speaker, business consultant, and award-winning author of the book *Moving from Activity to Achievement*. A veteran of the U.S. Navy, he often uses the principles of navigation to illustrate what business leaders must do to reach their desired goals. As an example, he cited the process NASA uses in getting a space vehicle from the launch pad to its destination when he wrote, "After a rocket launch, mission control . . . spends most of its time making adjustments to the course of the vehicle. . . . Each mission starts with an extensive written plan for successful completion. Then, from the time the space vehicle is launched until the moment it lands on target, NASA spends 99 percent of its time adjusting the flight plan. Because of unforeseen circumstances . . . adjustments must be made to the original plan."

Taylor also draws on his naval experiences to make his point. "We would spend weeks," he said, "charting a very detailed course from San Diego, California, to the South China Sea; but on each cruise, we found ourselves needing to make course adjustments, even before we were out of the harbor. As detailed as our plans might have been, and they were quite detailed, we still had to plan on making course adjustments.

"Whether trying to land a spacecraft on the moon or getting a ship from one port to another, course adjustments must be made. There are no exceptions."

In Larry Bossidy and Ram Charan's book *Execution,* coauthor Charan uses a slightly different analogy: "Leaders in an execution culture design strategies that are more road maps than rigid paths enshrined in fat planning books. That way, they can respond quickly when the unexpected happens. Their strategies are designed to be executed."

What does Charan mean by this? Well, a road map shows you the best route to take you from Point A to Point B via automobile travel; but road closures, accidents, or heavy traffic may dictate a change in strategy. While your destination remains the same, you may need to take alternate routes to get you there; in other words, to execute your plan.

Marketing coach and consultant Debra Murphy is the founder/principal of Massachusetts-based Masterful Marketing. In the December 29, 2008, entry in her blog (http://masterful-marketing.com/blog), she described the relationship between a marketing plan and the execution of that plan. She writes, "A great marketing plan is done to guide you in your marketing activities. The plan helps you understand how each activity works in synergy with your other marketing activities, and . . . ensures you give a consistent message throughout. But the real key to success in marketing is the ability to execute the plan."

## Execute Fast and Well

In his book, *The Marketing Manager's Handbook: The Keys to Sales and Marketing Success,* author Eric Gagnon emphasizes the importance of marketing execution. This director of Washington, DC–based Business

Marketing Institute writes, "Gaining the ability to execute fast and well not only means you get your marketing program under firm control, it also gives you the power to attack any promising new marketing opportunity that arises."

Gagnon outlines some of the common mistakes that marketing managers make, one of which is waiting in the hope that "something better" will come along. He explains that, "A well-executed marketing program that arrives in time to generate inquiries and sales for your company is infinitely more valuable than an even better one that is not there when needed; or is hobbled by rushed, slipshod, or late execution." Gagnon also has this advice for his readers, "Don't be afraid to 'fail faster.' Sometimes, the only way to learn the most effective way to sell your company's product is to suck it up and execute your plan."

## Thrilling the Customers

Grant Thornton LLP—U.S. member firm of six global audit, tax and advisory organizations known as Grant Thornton International—periodically conducts surveys of U.S. business leaders. In one such survey of 300 leaders from 2006, the firm took "an in-depth look at how business leaders are making execution central to their companies' success." The firm found that focusing on superior execution had become a priority among CEOs, with 83 percent listing it among their top three priorities. The report stated that, "Superior and consistent execution across all major business processes requires a special focus and commitment from the CEO."

The report concluded by saying, "In this survey, superior execution begins to emerge as a path to differentiation. Business leaders are not only looking at what their brands promise, but are also considering the importance of a superior and consistent execution of that promise. There is a sense that to really stand out and gain customer trust, companies must move beyond simply satisfying their customers to 'thrilling' them. For many customers, the thrill could be as straightforward as enjoying a quality experience that is flawlessly executed time and time again."

## Execute with Frequency

When you think of Geico, what do you think of? Perhaps their slogan, "15 minutes could save you 15 percent or more . . ." Or maybe that gecko lizard with the British accent comes to mind, or the stack of money with the eyeballs that seems to distract and attract everyone near it. Or maybe—just maybe—you think of all three! Geico has done a particularly remarkable job at grabbing attention for its insurance products. Frequency of their simple and somewhat annoying messages has brought them incredible brand awareness.

But what if you don't have millions to advertise your simple message to a national audience? That does limit you from national advertising, but it doesn't limit you from doing what Geico is doing at the core. They are simply repeating their message to their prospects with great frequency.

---

Do you frequently repeat your core benefits or offerings to your prospects?

_____

_____

_____

_____

---

## Take 15 and Get Your Clients Going Wild!
### A 15-Minute Client-Builder Exercise

What is the one strategy you will execute fully and with precision?

_____

_____

_____

_____

---

## In Other Words

*However beautiful the strategy, you should occasionally look at the results.*

—*Winston Churchill*

*Vision without execution is a hallucination.*

—*Thomas A. Edison*

*In preparing for battle I have always found that plans are useless, but planning is indispensable.*

—*Dwight D. Eisenhower*

*Waiting for perfect is never as smart as making progress.*

—*Seth Godin*

# The Playbook
# Online and Traditional
# Marketing Techniques

## CHAPTER 7

# Create a Playbook that Fits Your Business and Your Personality

## Design Your Own Marketing Action Plan

Firms that implement marketing successfully and consistently usually start with a plan. Large companies typically require extensive and detailed marketing plans, and small companies often have something less formal. But no matter the plan's size, in order for it to garner results, it needs to be thoughtfully designed; written down somewhere; action oriented (with dates and people assigned to tasks); implemented; and reviewed monthly with performance monitoring.

A long-term business plan with goals and financing, alliances, and vision is important; however, a typical marketing plan should include one year of strategy and activities. For small businesses, a one-year time frame is often the best period to plan marketing. Some items may extend beyond or be achieved after one year, but it can be a waste of time to plan in detail for three or five years of marketing activities in a flexible and sometimes fast-moving small firm.

A marketing plan is designed for your marketing staff to implement, but it also provides direction and confidence to company leadership and the entire staff. Share your plan with the entire organization so that others can understand your activities and the growth that is on the horizon.

This chapter provides a template for building out your marketing plan by using the forms throughout this book, as well as more valuable exercises. At the end of this chapter you will find an action plan template for you to record all of your marketing actions, dates, and people responsible for implementation in one place. A digital download of the action plan template (see Figure 7.1) can also be found at www.AndtheClientsWentWild.com. Enter the code: WILD to download the action plan template for free!

---

## Marketing Plan: Your Playbook for Winning All the Business You Want!

### Part I: Goals

List the successes you had in _____ (previous planning year)

ACCOMPLISHMENTS

- _____
- _____
- _____
- _____
- _____
- _____
- _____
- _____

ACTIONS THAT LEAD TO THE SUCCESSES:

- _____
- _____
- _____
- _____
- _____
- _____

**WHERE AM I?**

*Conduct a Complete Assessment of Your Situation by Asking Yourself:*

- How much growth have I had—in terms of income and number of clients—in the past year?

  _____

  _____

- Over the past three years?

  _____

  _____

- How have I obtained most of my clients to date?

  _____

  _____

- Which marketing strategies have worked well for me?

  _____

  _____

- Which ones haven't?

  _____

  _____

- How long have I had my typical client?

  _____

  _____

- What's my average revenue per client?

  _____

  _____

- What readily identifiable "niche," if any, do my clients fall into?

  _____

  _____

- What system, if any, do I have to ensure a steady flow of referrals?

  _____

  _____

- What changes do I need to make in the way I do business to be successful?

  _____

  _____

*(continued)*

(*continued*)

*Set Your Goals:*

1. _____
_____

2. _____
_____

3. _____
_____

4. _____
_____

5. _____
_____

6. Revenue of the business: _____

7. Number of new clients/customers: _____

8. Yearly value of new clients/customers: _____

9. Number of new prospects: _____

10. Number of appointments per week: _____

### Part II: Principles, Strategy, and Tactics
### First Principle—What Are You Doing that No One Else Is Doing? Build Client Delight Through Your Differentiation

What do people dislike most about your industry, service, or product offering? (for example, the bathrooms at gas stations)

_____
_____
_____
_____
_____
_____

Can you offer a solution to what people dislike most?

_____
_____
_____
_____
_____
_____
_____

What can you provide that is truly different?

_____
_____
_____
_____
_____
_____
_____

List an offering you could make that would surprise (and maybe even go viral)!

_____
_____
_____
_____
_____
_____

What is a "Freemium" you could offer?

_____
_____
_____
_____
_____
_____
_____

*(continued)*

*(continued)*

Who do you hire? What type of person do you want to hire?

_____
_____
_____
_____
_____
_____
_____

What could you provide that no one else has taken to market?

_____
_____
_____
_____
_____
_____
_____

Can you create a whole new category?

_____
_____
_____
_____
_____
_____
_____

What are you selling that you could promote in a unique way?

_____
_____
_____
_____
_____
_____

What can you offer or do that no one else will?

_____
_____
_____
_____

## WHAT WILL GET YOUR CLIENTS GOING WILD?

*List a different approach or offer that no one else is doing*

_____

_____

_____

_____

_____

_____

_____

*Action Steps (Transfer these to your Master Action Plan at the end of this chapter)*

Date                 Action

\_\_\_/\_\_\_/\_\_\_      _____

\_\_\_/\_\_\_/\_\_\_      _____

\_\_\_/\_\_\_/\_\_\_      _____

\_\_\_/\_\_\_/\_\_\_      _____

### *Second Principle—Focus Your Marketing on Benefits, Results, and a Call to Action: What's Really In It for Them*

## WHAT DO YOUR BEST CLIENTS WANT? WHAT RESULTS DO THEY CARE ABOUT?

_____

_____

_____

_____

_____

_____

_____

_____

*(continued)*

*(continued)*

*List the ways in which you currently promote your products and services*

| Product or Service | Feature | Compelling Benefit |
| --- | --- | --- |
| _____ | _____ | _____ |
| _____ | _____ | _____ |
| _____ | _____ | _____ |
| _____ | _____ | _____ |

## EVALUATE WHETHER YOUR CLIENTS AND PROSPECTS *TRULY* CARE ABOUT YOUR COMPELLING BENEFITS

_____

_____

_____

_____

_____

_____

_____

*List your current features and beside each list the result*

| Feature | Result |
| --- | --- |
| _____ | _____ |
| _____ | _____ |
| _____ | _____ |
| _____ | _____ |
| _____ | _____ |

## CONDUCT A MESSAGE STRATEGY SESSION

*Before you do any marketing, conduct your own Message Strategy Session with your team by asking one another:*

1. What is the *challenge* our product or service overcomes?

_____

_____

_____

_____

_____

2. What are the words our customers are using to describe *their challenge*?

   _____

   _____

   _____

   _____

   _____

   _____

3. What is our *solution* (using words they will relate to)?

   _____

   _____

   _____

   _____

   _____

4. What are the specific *benefits* of our product or service?

   _____

   _____

   _____

   _____

   _____

5. List your benefits with *clear messaging* for each targeted prospect

   _____

   _____

   _____

   _____

LIST YOUR MOST EFFECTIVE CALLS TO ACTION
(AND FUTURE ONES, TOO)

_____

_____

_____

_____

_____

_____

*(continued)*

(*continued*)

## WHAT WILL GET YOUR CLIENTS GOING WILD?

List your product or service's best benefit, compelling message, and call to action to buy

_____

_____

_____

_____

_____

_____

_____

_____

_____

Action Steps (*Transfer these to your Master Action Plan at the end of this chapter*)

Date            Action

___/___/___     _____

___/___/___     _____

___/___/___     _____

___/___/___     _____

___/___/___     _____

### Third Principle—Go Viral! Create Memorable Impactful Messaging Worthy of a Pass-Along

Consider what may be an "idea virus" in your business. List potential ideas that could have the power to spread from person to person to person.

_____

_____

_____

_____

_____

_____

*List possible affiliates that would be interested in your message*

_____

_____

_____

_____

_____

_____

_____

*Does your idea meet the four contagion factors? How?*

1. Strength of the message:

   _____

   _____

   _____

   _____

2. Size of the population of opportunity:

   _____

   _____

   _____

   _____

3. Potential number of days the message will be contagious:

   _____

   _____

   _____

   _____

4. Number of people message carriers have in their network:

   _____

   _____

   _____

   _____

*(continued)*

(continued)

## What Will Get Your Clients Going Wild?

*What viral campaigns can I create? List the idea, message, and how it could be distributed*

_____

_____

_____

_____

_____

_____

_____

Action Steps (Transfer these to your Master Action Plan at the end of this chapter)

Date                Action

__/__/__        _____

__/__/__        _____

__/__/__        _____

__/__/__        _____

__/__/__        _____

### Fourth Principle—Leverage Your Business Network for Incremental Growth: Find and Cultivate Centers of Influence to Move Your Message Fast

## Powerful Connections List

1. _____

2. _____

3. _____

4. _____

5. _____

6. _____

7. _____

8. _____
9. _____
10. _____
11. _____
12. _____
13. _____
14. _____
15. _____
16. _____
17. _____
18. _____
19. _____
20. _____

Continue to 100.

What are some innovative ways you can target and reach your potential advocates?

_____
_____
_____
_____
_____
_____
_____

*With what specific businesses might you create alliances?*

1. _____
2. _____
3. _____
4. _____
5. _____
6. _____
7. _____

*(continued)*

(*continued*)

*Groups you could join to build your own powerful network*

Charity _____

Church Group _____

Industry Group _____

Alumni Group _____

Rotary or other international organization _____

EO or other international entrepreneur organization with qualified entry standards _____

## FOUR STEPS TO LEVERAGE YOUR NEW BUSINESS VENTURE

1. Write out your vision of exactly what you want and need to be successful quickly.

   _____

   _____

   _____

   _____

   _____

2. Identify those who can connect you to what you most want and need. Search and connect as if you had no money—even if you do. A vision with no money needs great passion to survive.

   _____

   _____

   _____

   _____

   _____

3. Create a "What's In It for Them" plan to forge a leveraged relationship. List the reasons why each potential partner would want to work with you on your venture.

   _____

   _____

   _____

   _____

4. Begin reaching out in person, through the phone and via e-mail with your prepared plan to create win-win relationships.

Get your business off the ground with little to no start-up capital if possible; and keep in mind that the best capital is your connections.

_____

_____

_____

_____

_____

*List the ways in which you delight your clients:*

_____

_____

_____

_____

_____

_____

## WHAT WILL GET YOUR CLIENTS GOING WILD?

*Record your best leveraging strategy action item*

_____

_____

_____

_____

_____

_____

*Action Steps (Transfer these to your Master Action Plan at the end of this chapter)*

Date                    Action

___/___/___        _____

___/___/___        _____

___/___/___        _____

___/___/___        _____

___/___/___        _____

*(continued)*

*(continued)*

### *Fifth Principle—The Critical Importance of Execution in Your Game Plan: Good Execution Is Better than Good Strategy*

How much time and effort will you allocate each week to your marketing strategies?

_____
_____
_____
_____
_____
_____
_____

How will you evaluate and review your marketing strategies to ensure effective execution?

_____
_____
_____
_____
_____
_____
_____

### WHAT WILL GET YOUR CLIENTS GOING WILD?

*What is the one strategy you will execute fully and with precision?*

_____
_____
_____
_____
_____
_____

*Action Steps (Transfer these to your Master Action Plan at the end of this chapter)*

Date              Action

___/___/___      _____
___/___/___      _____
___/___/___      _____

## BUILD A BRAND IDENTITY ON SHOESTRING BUDGET: SPENDING TIME EFFECTIVELY CAN BE WORTH MORE THAN MONEY

How do you think your clients describe your brand?

_____

_____

_____

_____

_____

## THE FIVE ATTRIBUTES OF A STRONG BRAND

1. Delivers benefits that the clients want.

   What benefits do your clients and prospects want?

   _____

   _____

   _____

   _____

   _____

   _____

2. Consistency in quality.

   What is the quality perception that your clients have? Ask them!

   _____

   _____

   _____

   _____

   _____

   _____

3. Price.

   What is your pricing strategy in good and not-so-good times?

   _____

   _____

   _____

   _____

   _____

   _____

   _____

*(continued)*

(*continued*)

4. The brand message remains consistent.

Is your brand consistent across the board? List all the mediums you have messaging and confirm the brand is projected the same everywhere.

_____

_____

_____

_____

_____

_____

_____

_____

_____

_____

5. The brand encompasses many marketing elements.

How many branding elements do you have (logo, slogan, signage, and packaging), and where do they appear?

_____

_____

_____

_____

_____

_____

_____

_____

_____

## WHAT WILL GET YOUR CLIENTS GOING WILD?

*How do I want my brand defined by others?*

_____

_____

_____

_____

*Action Steps (Transfer these to your Master Action Plan at the end of this chapter)*

Date    Action

___/___/___  _____

___/___/___  _____

___/___/___  _____

___/___/___  _____

___/___/___  _____

## FIND YOUR NICHE: CORNER THE MARKET ONE SEGMENT AT A TIME!

*List the specific niches you will target and why*

- _____
- _____
- _____
- _____

## WHAT WILL GET YOUR CLIENTS GOING WILD?

*List your focused activities within each target niche*

_____

_____

_____

_____

*Action Steps (Transfer these to your Master Action Plan at the end of this chapter)*

Date    Action

___/___/___  _____

___/___/___  _____

___/___/___  _____

___/___/___  _____

___/___/___  _____

*(continued)*

(*continued*)

TECHNIQUES FOR CREATING A MEMORABLE EXPERIENCE: GIVE 'EM SOMETHING TO TALK ABOUT!

What are the aspects of your business that people will want to talk about it?

_____
_____
_____
_____
_____
_____
_____
_____
_____

How do you regularly keep in touch with your best clients?

_____
_____
_____
_____
_____
_____
_____
_____

*List your 20 best clients*

1. _____
2. _____
3. _____
4. _____
5. _____
6. _____
7. _____
8. _____

9. _____

10. _____

11. _____

12. _____

13. _____

14. _____

15. _____

16. _____

17. _____

18. _____

19. _____

20. _____

What do you want your clients to do?

_____

_____

_____

_____

_____

_____

_____

_____

What are possible deliverable documents that will tell clients what you do?

_____

_____

_____

_____

_____

_____

_____

_____

*(continued)*

(*continued*)

*What service experiences can you offer to your clients?*

- _____
- _____
- _____
- _____
- _____
- _____
- _____

## WHAT WILL GET YOUR CLIENTS GOING WILD?

*What are the experiences you will create for your clients?*

_____

_____

_____

_____

_____

_____

_____

*Action Steps (Transfer these to your Master Action Plan at the end of this chapter)*

| Date | Action |
|------|--------|
| __/__/__ | _____ |
| __/__/__ | _____ |
| __/__/__ | _____ |
| __/__/__ | _____ |
| __/__/__ | _____ |

Your best prospects come from referrals, scripts, and strategies for increasing your introductions to others.

Create a "Who We Serve" list of the types of people who are good clients for you, their needs, and how you can help them. Show this list to clients. It is an effective method for helping the client think of qualified people to refer to you instead of giving the typical response: "I don't know anyone."

## Who We Serve

| Client Type | Need | Solution |
|---|---|---|
| _____ | _____ | _____ |
| _____ | _____ | _____ |
| _____ | _____ | _____ |
| _____ | _____ | _____ |
| _____ | _____ | _____ |
| _____ | _____ | _____ |

List the strategies you will use to generate referrals from new and existing clients:

_____

_____

_____

_____

_____

_____

_____

*List the best referral sources*

Clients? _____

Prospects? _____

Employees? _____

Colleagues? _____

Family and Friends? _____

Vendors? _____

Business and Professional Associations? _____

Social Contacts? _____

How will you request referrals?

_____

_____

_____

_____

_____

_____

_____

*(continued)*

(*continued*)

How will you thank those that give referrals?

_____

_____

_____

_____

_____

_____

_____

## WHAT WILL GET YOUR CLIENTS GOING WILD?

*List your best referral strategy for this year*

_____

_____

_____

_____

_____

_____

*Action Steps (Transfer these to your Master Action Plan at the end of this chapter)*

| Date | Action |
|------|--------|
| __/__/__ | _____ |
| __/__/__ | _____ |
| __/__/__ | _____ |
| __/__/__ | _____ |
| __/__/__ | _____ |

*My web site is working! Turn a bland site and your internet presence into a moneymaker.*

What benefits do you highlight on your home page?

_____

_____

_____

_____

_____

_____

What video content could you add to your web site?

_____

_____

_____

_____

_____

_____

_____

*Web Site Checklist*

Is my site reaching my target audience?                            ☐

Are the key elements in my site impactful?                         ☐

Are my product and service benefits clearly identified?            ☐

What are the elements that distinguish my company
from the competition on the site?                                  ☐

What are my calls to action?                                       ☐

What changes will you make to your web site right now?

_____

_____

_____

_____

_____

_____

_____

_____

_____

What changes will you make to your web site over the next year?

_____

_____

_____

_____

_____

_____

_____

_____

*(continued)*

(*continued*)

How will your prospects see the site (Search Engine Optimization)?

_____
_____
_____
_____
_____
_____
_____

What potential affiliates could drive traffic to your web site?

_____
_____
_____
_____
_____
_____
_____

## WHAT WILL GET YOUR CLIENTS GOING WILD?

*What element in my site will stop people in their tracks?*

_____
_____
_____
_____
_____
_____

*Action Steps (Transfer these to your Master Action Plan at the end of this chapter)*

Date                Action

__/__/__        _____
__/__/__        _____
__/__/__        _____
__/__/__        _____
__/__/__        _____

**Social Media:** Effective Strategies that *Don't* Consume All of Your Time

*List interesting content you could begin sharing online*

_____

_____

_____

_____

_____

_____

_____

*List your priority mediums for updates and follow up (Facebook, LinkedIn, Twitter, etc.)*

1. _____
2. _____
3. _____
4. _____
5. _____

*Select your brand management tracking tools and methods (Google Alerts, Technorati, Social Oomph, etc.)*

1. _____
2. _____
3. _____

*Determine the time you will spend using social media*

By setting specific days and times to focus on social media, you will be able to add in social media marketing effectively without it taking over your day, or worse, having it get pushed aside for days.

☐ *Weekly?* (Set Time) _____

– Or –

☐ *Daily?* (Set Time) _____

– Or –

☐ *Multiple Times Daily* (Set Times) _____

(continued)

*(continued)*

**WHAT WILL GET YOUR CLIENTS GOING WILD?**
*Once a month, review and discuss effectiveness of your Social Media activities*

_____

_____

_____

_____

_____

_____

_____

*Action Steps (Transfer these to your Master Action Plan at the end of this chapter)*

Date                Action

___/___/___          _____

___/___/___          _____

___/___/___          _____

___/___/___          _____

___/___/___          _____

**Permission Based Marketing:** Strategies for Successful E-Mail and E-Newsletters

Plan your e-mail newsletter by focusing on target, message, value, and frequency. Write out your objectives and your plan for reaching them.

_____

_____

_____

_____

_____

_____

_____

_____

**WHAT WILL GET YOUR CLIENTS GOING WILD?**
*What will get people looking forward to reading your e-mail mewsletter?*

_____

_____

_____

_____

_____

*Action Steps (Transfer these to your Master Action Plan at the end of this chapter)*

Date                    Action

___/___/___         _____

___/___/___         _____

___/___/___         _____

___/___/___         _____

___/___/___         _____

**Traditional Marketing Still Works:** TV and Cable Advertising, Newspaper, and Other Mediums that Still Cause People to Buy

How will you track the success of your marketing activities?

_____

_____

_____

_____

Who is your advertising target?

_____

_____

_____

_____

*(continued)*

(*continued*)

Do the demographics of the medium's audience meet your target?
_____
_____
_____
_____
_____

List your impactful message requesting specific and direct action.
_____
_____
_____
_____
_____

Where do your customers live? How can you reach them directly?
_____
_____
_____
_____
_____

What can you do in your regular advertising and promotion using the techniques that make infomercials work?
_____
_____
_____
_____
_____
_____

1. Tell a story and show the product in action.
_____
_____
_____

2. Layer it with powerful customer testimonials.

   _____

   _____

   _____

   _____

3. Have strong and continuous calls to action.

   _____

   _____

   _____

   _____

4. Overcome objections (again and again).

   _____

   _____

   _____

   _____

Would an infomercial be an option for your product or service? If so, what is your next step to put it into action?

_____

_____

_____

_____

_____

_____

_____

### WHAT WILL GET YOUR CLIENTS GOING WILD?

*Create a plan for successful advertising, including what you will sell, your compelling message and call to action, and testing and tracking techniques.*

_____

_____

_____

_____

_____

_____

_____

*(continued)*

(*continued*)

*Action Steps (Transfer these to your Master Action Plan at the end of this chapter)*

Date                        Action

___/___/___        _____

___/___/___        _____

___/___/___        _____

___/___/___        _____

___/___/___        _____

*Direct Mail: Simple Principles for Gaining Sales from Good Old-Fashioned Mail*

   A Simple Direct Mail Formula

1. Revenue goal that you want your mailing to produce  _____
   _____

2. Average sale amount of product/service _____
   _____

3. Enter your closing ratio (If 100 customers are interested in the product and 50 end up buying it, your closing ratio is 50 percent) _____
   _____

4. Estimate your mailing response rate. (Most direct mail campaigns produce a 0.5 percent–2 percent response) _____
   _____

   Enter your numbers in the calculation:

Avg. Sale ___ × Close Ratio ___ × Response Rate ___ =
___/Revenue Goal _____ = # to mail

What design elements will you use to get your message to stand out?

_____

_____

_____

_____

_____

What's your offer?

_____

_____

_____

_____

_____

What is your target audience for your mailing?

_____

_____

_____

_____

_____

What response vehicle(s) will you have?

_____

_____

_____

_____

_____

How will you test your strategy?

_____

_____

_____

_____

_____

*Measure Your Responses*

Keep detailed reports on the following data:

1. Number of pieces mailed
2. Number of responses you received
3. Response source
4. Conversion percentage
5. Income those responses generate
6. Average order
7. Percentage response
8. Cost per order or cost per response

(*continued*)

(continued)

9. Net profit

10. Returns and bad debt

## WHAT WILL GET YOUR CLIENTS GOING WILD?

*Plan your next direct mail campaign using the five key elements: Design, Message, Target, Response Vehicle, and Strategy Test. When will you start? What are your objectives?*

_____

_____

_____

_____

_____

_____

*Action Steps (Transfer these to your Master Action Plan at the end of this chapter)*

Date            Action

__/__/__        _____

__/__/__        _____

__/__/__        _____

__/__/__        _____

__/__/__        _____

**Events and Seminars:** Creating Buzz and Sales Through Group Presentations

*Calendar of Public Events/Seminars*

- _____
- _____
- _____
- _____
- _____
- _____

**WHAT WILL GET YOUR CLIENTS GOING WILD?**
*Create events that will show your value and get people talking!*

_____

_____

_____

_____

_____

_____

_____

*Action Steps (Transfer these to your Master Action Plan at the end of this chapter)*

Date                Action

__/__/__          _____

__/__/__          _____

__/__/__          _____

__/__/__          _____

__/__/__          _____

**Media Methods to Gain Celebrity Status:** Take advantage of hot topics, timely events, and unique twists to attract attention.

How often will you submit a press release or article to the media?

_____

_____

_____

_____

_____

_____

What topics can you write about that the media may be interested in?

_____

_____

_____

_____

_____

*(continued)*

(*continued*)

## WHAT WILL GET YOUR CLIENTS GOING WILD?

*What media outlet will you focus on that could be potentially "Game Changing" if they were exposed to your unique value?*

_____

_____

_____

_____

_____

_____

_____

*Action Steps (Transfer these to your Master Action Plan at the end of this chapter)*

| Date | Action |
|------|--------|
| __/__/__ | _____ |
| __/__/__ | _____ |
| __/__/__ | _____ |
| __/__/__ | _____ |
| __/__/__ | _____ |

## USE THIS WORKSHEET TO PLAN AND EVALUATE YOUR MARKETING PROJECTS

*Marketing Action Worksheet*

Project: _____

Objectives: _____

Budget: _____

Target: _____

Marketing Medium(s): _____

General Message: _____

Implementation Timeline: _____

Date                    Action

___/___/___     _____

___/___/___     _____

___/___/___     _____

___/___/___     _____

___/___/___     _____

*Marketing*
## Action Plan

| COMPLETED | START DATE | COMPLETION DATE DUE | PROJECT | PERSON(S) RESPONSIBLE | BUDGET |
|---|---|---|---|---|---|
| **MARKETING CATEGORY** _____ | | | | | |
|  |  |  |  |  |  |
|  |  |  |  |  |  |
|  |  |  |  |  |  |
| **MARKETING CATEGORY** _____ | | | | | |
|  |  |  |  |  |  |
|  |  |  |  |  |  |
|  |  |  |  |  |  |
| **MARKETING CATEGORY** _____ | | | | | |
|  |  |  |  |  |  |
|  |  |  |  |  |  |
|  |  |  |  |  |  |
| **MARKETING CATEGORY** _____ | | | | | |
|  |  |  |  |  |  |
|  |  |  |  |  |  |
|  |  |  |  |  |  |
| **MARKETING CATEGORY** _____ | | | | | |
|  |  |  |  |  |  |
|  |  |  |  |  |  |
|  |  |  |  |  |  |

**Figure 7.1    Master Action Plan**

Copyright © 2010 by Red Zone Marketing

## CHAPTER 8

# Build a Brand Identity on a Shoestring Budget

## Spending Time Effectively Can Be Worth More than Money

*Your brand is ultimately what your clients say about you.*

According to integrated marketing specialist Karl Schaller, "The brand craze of a few years ago signaled the beginning of a marketing communications revolution [that is] now coming to full bloom across the country." This revolution has caused businesses, professional firms, associations, and even nonprofit organizations to place greater emphasis on branding than ever before.

"It's no longer good enough to be good enough," warns Seth Godin, successful entrepreneur and author of numerous books, including best-selling *Purple Cow.* "Only the exceptional, the amazing, and the remarkable have a chance to build awareness, word of mouth, and profits."

The American Marketing Association defines branding as: "a name, term, sign, symbol or design, or a combination of [these] intended to identify the goods and services of one seller or group of sellers and to differentiate them from those of other sellers."

Branding, then, essentially means image-building. Professor of marketing and leading thinker in the field, Dr. David Aakers defines branding as, "the internalized sum of all impressions received by a consumer, which results in a distinctive position in their minds based on perceived emotional and functional benefits."

The key word here is "distinctive." Duane Knapp, a pioneer in the field of brain science and author of *The Brain Mindset* and *The Brain Promise* echoes that theme. "The key to thinking like a genuine brand," he writes, "is [to understand] the requirement to be distinctive. It's not an optional kind of idea. It's not possible to have a genuine brand without achieving the perception of being distinctive."

What I have observed in all businesses, but most prominently in small businesses, is that your brand is essentially what *your clients* say about you, not what *you* say about you. Though promotion, advertising, and marketing can build your message, your customers ultimately define what your brand and perception in the marketplace really is based on different attributes. Your brand is *not* your logo, tag line, or "elevator speech"; it is how someone else describes you, your firm, your staff, and what you offer. The good news is that strengthening your brand with your clients is an inexpensive and highly profitable form of marketing.

## Your Clients Already Describe Your Brand (As They See It)

Your exposure within your target market determines much of your success. The stronger your brand, the more credible and visible you are, and the easier it becomes for others to do business with you. You control your brand through your clients almost entirely through your communication. Impactful contact with customers leads to confidence and trust. It differentiates you from competitors, makes your clients feel important, gives them something to talk about, and brings in the referrals you deserve.

Do you think you've made a memorable impression in the minds of your clients (and potential clients)—one that sets you apart from others who do the same thing that your firm does? If you want your clients to go *wild* about you, they must be able to clearly define what distinguishes your offerings. After all, you don't usually get excited about the more mundane features of a firm. Your clients are the leading source for answering what your firm is all about.

How do you think your clients describe your brand?

_____

_____

_____

_____

## A Coast-to-Coast Billboard

It takes considerable effort to achieve uniqueness in the marketplace, especially when potential customers are bombarded thousands of times daily with promotional messages that come at us from every direction. Gary Ruskin, former executive director of Commercial Alert, a Washington, DC–based nonprofit organization whose stated mission is "to keep the commercial culture within its proper sphere," told one interviewer that, "There's an effort to turn every square inch of this country into a billboard."

Although "every square inch" might sound somewhat extreme, based on some reports I've read, Ruskin was not exaggerating. Several years ago, for example, well-known author and journalist Mitch Albom interviewed a couple that had decided to sell the rights to name their newborn son to the highest commercial bidder with bids starting at $500,000. The father assured Albom that "We have standards," and that the only unacceptable products would be guns and cigarettes. To date, I have seen no follow-up reports, so I can't pass along the name of the winning organization, if any, or the amount it paid.

Another individual decided to use his head—literally—as an advertising medium, listing his forehead for rent on eBay. Sure enough, he found a taker. The CEO of one company, noting that the young man "clearly has a head for business," paid him $37,375 to display its logo on his forehead—for one month!

Far-fetched examples? Sure they are! Over the top? Of course! But the message they convey is clear: getting heard above the incessant "Ask your doctor if (fill in the blank) is right for you"; "not available in stores"; and the "But wait, there's more!" claims becomes more and more difficult every single day.

In such a tough environment, developing a unique and memorable brand is more challenging and important than ever before. Legendary advertising executive Bruce Barton once warned that, "An election goes on every minute of the business day . . . where the customers state their preferences and determine which manufacturer and which product shall be the leader today and which shall lead tomorrow."

Barton uttered these words more than 40 years ago, but the only revision I'd suggest to make it more applicable in today's world would be to change "every minute of the business day" to "every minute of the day and night." It is indeed a 24/7 world, in which the drumbeat never stops and the need to stand out from the crowd is essential. In the words of branding and creative marketing consultant Dick Bruso, "The process of creating a distinctive brand takes time and commitment, but needs to be a top priority." Bruso is the founder and principal of Colorado-based Heard Above the Noise, a firm that specializes in helping clients identify and build their unique brands.

Nonprofit executive David Rendall takes the process a step further by claiming that, "Branding is essentially concerned with five key areas: message, purpose, audience, image, and promise. A good brand should proclaim a specific purpose to a certain audience in order to create a clearly defined *image* and it must be able to deliver on what it *promises*. Branding and brand management are the process of influencing a market through the *message* a brand creates."

Create the right image for your business—it is critical to your success. Consider the fact that more than half of all new independent businesses fail in the first five years of existence. Conversely, more than 75 percent of those who open a franchised business find success in that same period. What accounts for such a large difference? Much of it clearly has to do with the standard and well-proven operating systems developed by the franchisor, but a great deal of credit for the higher success rate comes from the buying public's instant recognition of the particular brand or image.

## Image Is Everything

Early in his career, tennis star Andre Agassi was featured in a series of commercials for Canon cameras, declaring in each of them that, "Image is everything." It turned out to be quite an ironic statement, because his 2009 autobiography *Open* describes a life in which Agassi attempted to create an image that was not at all who he really was.

Image may not be *everything* in your marketing activities, but it can and should be the foundation. Another legendary advertising executive, David Ogilvy, said, "You have to decide what 'image' you want for your brand. Image means personality. Products, like people, have personalities, and they can make or break them in the marketplace."

Your goal in your business should be to *own your market*. Create a consistent image around your product or service. Differentiate yourself from your competitors with an extraordinary business image; for example, something like the Nike Swoosh. It fits anywhere, even on something as small as a golf ball, but is instantly recognizable. Find a similarly clear image that communicates *your* product or service immediately, and explains why someone should buy it. Your name, logo, products, services, unique selling proposition (USP), and ancillary offerings must all speak the same language and project a unified message.

## Separate Yourself from Your Competitors

Why should people do business with you instead of with a competitor? Well, they probably won't, unless you have something that the other company doesn't have—some kind of benefit for the buyer. For example, you want a new marketing brochure designed and printed. Company A will do the entire job for $75 an hour, with a $600 nonrefundable advance, and no guarantee of how many hours the job might take. Company B will do the same job for a predetermined "not to exceed" cost, with no down payment, plus a guarantee that unless you're completely satisfied, there'll be no fee. Both companies do quality work, and the turnaround time is roughly the same. But Company B has a USP that gives it a distinct advantage over its competitor; and chances are that's the company you'll select to do your brochure.

## What's In a Name?

The branding strategy begins with a seemingly simple part of your business: your name. Does your business name and image immediately reveal what you do? Think about what you're communicating, who your target is, and what you want to accomplish. Take a look at the business listings in the white pages of your local telephone directory and try and figure out what many of those companies do. You'll find names like The Morgan Company, Brown & Associates, Smith & Green, The Anderson Group, Todd's Inc., and Julianne's. These names say nothing about what these companies do, or who their audiences might be.

Your name should immediately convey who you are and establish that you're different. For example, a number of years ago an associate of mine who is a writer launched his own business, which he named Kelly Communications, Inc. The name said nothing about who the company is or what it does. It did not convey a unique image or offering. After repeatedly having to explain to people that he wasn't in telecommunications or similar fields, he changed the name of his business to WordCrafters, Inc., and the questions about what he does for a living evaporated.

When I started my own business, I could have called it Kuzmeski & Associates—which doesn't tell you a thing. Instead, I named it Red Zone Marketing. The Red Zone Marketing logo and the trademark behind it appear on everything I do. All the presentations I make and the book you're currently reading all carry the Red Zone theme.

## You Don't Have to Break the Bank to Develop Your Brand

In developing your image, or brand, avoid gimmicks; instead, focus on an image that's memorable, and be sure to use it consistently throughout every phase of your operation. Branding is not simply another name for marketing and/or advertising. It is a great deal more, although those two factors are definitely part of the mix. And organizations and individuals *don't* have to break the bank to develop a successful brand. In fact, the explosive growth of Social Media Marketing (SMM)—sites like LinkedIn, Facebook, Twitter, and so forth—make it possible for nearly everyone to have a chance at developing a successful brand on a shoestring budget.

Gary Vaynerchuk, cofounder of New Jersey–based retail wine business Wine Library, is a case in point. By taking advantage of social media marketing and other web-based tools, he has seen his business grow from annual sales of $4 million less than a decade ago to about $50 million today.

For example, more than 80,000 viewers tune in to Vaynerchuk's Wine Library TV program daily. "Viral aspects of your message explode once you use these tools," he said. "When I think about how much brand equity I have with Wine Library TV and how quickly it happened, the fact that I spent millions of dollars building the brand prior to using these tools makes me want to throw up."

(You can find detailed information about developing successful SMM strategies in Chapter 10, "Techniques for Creating a Memorable Experience.")

## Managing Your Brand Online

You must first believe that online branding is important—and for most businesses it is! The work you put into developing your online reputation and strengthening your brand has never been more important to your company's image than it is today. And your work online is not "playing around." It is conducting business the way it's being done today, both on land and online. Also, it is far less costly than any other form of marketing. It does take time; however, it is time well spent!

A first step to take here is to visit the site for Google Alerts (www.google .com/alerts) and set up a search on Twitter (you can use www.TweetDeck .com) to find out what people are saying—both good and bad—about you and your competitors. Searching and online communicating is an in-demand new job position at many firms. The staff member who does this at Red Zone Marketing is our "Director of Online Reputation," and she actually has one of the most critical positions in the company. She's not only working to get brand exposure online, but also responding and communicating with others who are discussing the brand.

## The Five Attributes of a Strong Brand

Building and properly managing a brand continues to be a significant priority for companies both large and small. The reason? From a strong brand comes client loyalty and significantly higher profits. The sections below outline the five attributes of successful and strong brands.

### 1. *Delivers Benefits that the Clients Want*

Customers don't buy a product simply because it is the "best." It is a combination of the quality of the product, the service, the image, location, and other factors. For instance, I probably wouldn't say to someone that I buy Kellogg's Rice Krispies because of the ads on TV or because of its lower shelf location at the store. I would probably say that I buy it for the taste, because that is logical. But truthfully, there may be a combination of reasons that I reach for that cereal when in the grocery store—taste, value, packaging, messaging, price, and the image I have of the cereal. These are all things I've determined that I want in a cereal, because although there

What benefits do your clients and prospects want?

_____

_____

_____

_____

are many other choices that may taste as good as Rice Krispies, I keep going back to the same brand. Is your brand delivering what your clients and prospects really want? Do you know exactly what that is?

## 2.   Maintains Consistency in Quality

A strong brand is connected to quality, but it is also the perception of the product, the people who use the product, when and why they use it, and the feeling people have about the product. The strongest brands focus on maintaining quality while altering their perceptions through messaging to fit the times.

---

What is the quality perception that your clients have? If you don't know—ask them!

_____

_____

_____

_____

---

## 3.   Pricing Strategy

A too high—or even too low—price point can dramatically affect your brand. If Louis Vuitton purses sold for $20 (as they often do illegally on the streets of New York!) or in discount retailers, the brand certainly wouldn't have the image of an upscale designer. But price and value are two different things, and value is far more important than price. Value includes quality, price, convenience, and reliability. Sometimes a lower price isn't better because people are seeking the better product for their needs. But when economic times get uncertain, pricing becomes more important.

In 2009, grocery stores in the Chicago area (and all over the country) slashed prices to attract consumers looking for relief from the high cost of feeding a family. Stores like Dominick's Finer Foods, Jewel-Osco, and Meijer's cut prices 20 percent to 30 percent on thousands of items because of the economic troubles. In an interview with _Progressive Grocer_ magazine in October 2009, Meijer's EVP of merchandising, J. K. Symancyk, said, "The current economic climate has created a generation of very strategic shoppers. It's incumbent on us to make it as easy as possible to shop our stores, and to communicate the fact that our customers are getting the lowest prices."

When times are difficult, brand equity can be improved by pricing strategies. Convenience and other criteria may become less important. Firms need to be flexible with price, while simultaneously continuing to protect their brand. And the only way to do this is stay in touch with your customers, watch your competitors, and make the best decisions given the information you have.

What is your pricing strategy in good times and not-so-good times?

_____

_____

_____

_____

## 4. The Brand Message Remains Consistent

Every interaction a customer has with your brand must be integrated across all marketing channels. How consistently do you communicate your brand's meaning? Do the messages of your various marketing programs conflict? For example, your web site content and e-mail campaigns should be fully incorporated with your offline efforts. All should proclaim a single, clear branding message and design throughout. The variety of marketing efforts could easily confuse customers, send conflicting messages—and result in a fractioned brand.

Is your brand message consistent across the board? List all the mediums you have communicating, and confirm that the brand is projected the same everywhere.

_____

_____

_____

_____

## 5. The Brand Encompasses Many Marketing Elements

A brand is made up of all marketing elements you have—including your logos, slogans, signage, packaging, and so on. Merely slapping your logo on your business cards and web sites may not be enough to spread your message. Strong brands display these images in many different places to enhance and reinforce consumer awareness. Apple, for instance, has its apple logo literally everywhere, including on their computers, iPods, and iPhones, to their promotions, advertising, and online. It is one of the most recognized logos in the world.

You may not have millions to spend on getting your logo everywhere, but where is it now? Where is your brand represented and how?

---

How many branding elements do you have (logo, slogan, signage, and packaging), and where do they appear?

_____

_____

_____

_____

---

## A Strong Brand with All of These Attributes—Plus One More

A strong following for a brand is sometimes called a "cult following." This phrase is typically used when referring to a small or large group of fans that are either somewhat or highly dedicated to a specific product or issue.

In 1982, David Yurman—a privately held high-end jewelry designer—introduced what has become the company's signature item: the cable bracelet. This iconic style remains Yurman's most popular piece to this day, even though the company has gone on to produce various jewelry and watch collections for men and women, as well as Yurman's own signature fragrance and eyewear collection. It was the cable design that set off the first of the now millions of loyal and fanatic Yurman followers.

I received a small David Yurman necklace as a gift a few years ago. I was familiar with the brand, but did not yet own a piece. I'm continually surprised at the reaction I get when wearing the rather modest necklace. Whenever—and I really mean *whenever*—I wear the necklace, at least one person comments on it. I get stopped by women who say, "I love your Yurman—I have several pieces too—see. . . ." I have been stopped by men who say, "Is that David Yurman? My wife loves Yurman!" I even have a few pictures of myself in the necklace, on which people have even commented via e-mail.

David Yurman's best attribute? Word of mouth. By focusing on a noticeable and very consistent look for their jewelry, they have been able to create a buzz around their brand. The company was started by David and Sybil Yurman, and began as a small family business that took its creative designs to the public with incredible consistency. You can tell every piece of jewelry that is a Yurman simply by glancing at it. The brand and consistent look are also well known on the pages of fashion magazines like *Vogue*, *Harper's Bazaar*, and *Town & Country*, when worn by supermodels like Kate Moss and others.

Today, there are 18 David Yurman boutiques across 10 states, and four boutiques across three international cities. Their first international store was opened in Hong Kong's International Finance Center, with the brand's Asia headquarters nearby.

## The Power of Celebrity Attached to Your Brand

Many companies tie their image and brand to celebrities in the worlds of entertainment and sports, or simply to plain folks like Jared Fogle. Jared who? Why, for the past 10 years or so, he's been the central figure in the advertising campaigns for Subway restaurants. It seems that Jared once weighed in at 425 pounds. After switching his diet to Subway subs for lunch and dinner, he eventually shed more than 240 pounds, and became famous as Subway's spokesman.

Recently, however, photos of a newly enlarged Jared have begun appearing of various web sites, leaving Subway in an awkward position. This apparently came to light not long after Subway signed up Olympic swimming champion Michael Phelps, shortly before photos surfaced showing him puffing marijuana. Subway thus found itself with not just one but *two* issues affecting its image.

The list of falling and fallen stars is a long one, but perhaps the most notorious one of all has just recently and unexpectedly been uncovered— the fall from grace of the world's most famous golfer, Tiger Woods. Until recently, Woods was known not only for his unprecedented skills on the golf course, but as a husband and the father of two little ones. Then he wrecked his car late one night, shortly after an article in *National Enquirer* reported that he had been unfaithful to his wife. His world began to unravel. As of this writing, multiple young women have come forward claiming to have had affairs with Woods. The damage to his car was nothing compared to the damage done to the Tiger image and brand. How it will impact the images of Nike, Gatorade, and other companies that have endorsed him—and the extent to which they will continue to link his name with theirs—still isn't clear.

At the risk of sounding cynical, I suggest that if you're thinking about linking your brand and image to a personality, your safest course might be to bypass celebrities and hitch your wagon to a gecko, or perhaps to a team of Clydesdales. Or, simply, to yourself.

---

## Take 15 and Get Your Clients Going Wild!
### A 15-Minute Client-Builder Exercise

How do I want my brand defined?

_____

_____

_____

_____

---

## In Other Words

*A brand for a company is like a reputation for a person. You earn reputation by trying to do hard things well.*

—Jeff Bezos

*Leverage your brand. You shouldn't let two guys in a garage eat your shorts.*

—Guy Kawasaki

*You can't move up if you don't stand out. Regardless of age, regardless of position, regardless of the business we happen to be in, all of us need to understand the importance of branding.*

—Tom Peters

## CHAPTER 9.

# Find Your Niche

## Corner the Market One Segment at a Time!

Many years ago, then-president Charles Brower of advertising agency Batton, Barton, Durstine & Osborn (BBD&O) wrote that, "There is no such thing as 'soft sell' and 'hard sell.' There is only 'smart sell' and 'stupid sell.'" May I suggest that those business and professional men and women who see the whole world as their marketplace and who try to be all things to all people probably fit into that latter category.

How much better it is, then, to follow the advice of the industrialist and philanthropist Andrew Carnegie, who said, "I believe the true road to preeminent success in any line is to make yourself master of that line." In other words, the key to success is *specialization*—or *niche positioning*.

### Playing Your Position

The word "niche" is defined as "a place or position suitable or appropriate for a person . . ." as well as "a situation or activity suited to a person's ability." Interestingly, the word itself is derived from the French *se nicher*, which is translated as "to build a nest." Finding your niche—whether it is sports, personal hobbies, and pastimes, or the business and professional world—is exactly that: building your nest.

In the early days of professional football, every player was on the field for almost the entire game, playing both offense and defense. There were no such things as "special teams," or designated punters, place kickers, or kick returners. Substitutions were limited by rule and were few and far between. The 11 players on the field were expected to do it all.

Many players did indeed excel on both offense and defense. Among the best of them all was Sammy Baugh, who played for the National Football League's Washington Redskins from 1937 to 1952. Known as "Slingin' Sammy"—and a charter member of the Pro Football Hall of Fame—Baugh played both quarterback and defensive back, and did the team's punting as well. During several of his years with the team, he led the league both in passing and punting. In 1943, he accomplished the unprecedented feat of leading the league in three categories: passing, punting, and interceptions. In other words, Baugh was outstanding in the areas of offense (passing), defense (interceptions), and as a specialist (punting).

When Baugh was first approached by the Redskins after graduating from college, he was offered a salary of $4,000—not per game, but for the entire season! Instead, Baugh asked for—and received—$8,000, a tiny fraction of the seven-figure salaries paid to today's players, all of whom are specialists. Incidentally, that $8,000 figure made him the team's highest paid player at the time!

Many years later—when the rules of football were changed to allow unlimited substitutions—specialization became the order of the day in all levels of football. Today, no player can be both a great quarterback and a great wide receiver. Successful National Football League players have honed their skills at a particular position for many years, perhaps starting as early as grade school. A young man who has played linebacker all through high school and college doesn't suddenly decide he's going to become a quarterback when an NFL team drafts him. He's long since found his niche, and was selected in the draft because of his success in that position.

The same is true in business. To maximize your chances of success—to "score" regularly—you must focus on a particular niche, rather than trying to be all things to all people. This strategy will help you use your time more efficiently and effectively, will provide the highest return on investment, and will yield a stream of qualified referrals. Figure out who you enjoy working with, what need you can fulfill, and where you can add value—then, just do it! You'll find yourself in the red zone much more often, and will greatly increase your opportunities to score.

Once you find the right niche, one of the best ways to succeed is to position yourself as an expert in that area. You may have already established yourself in one area, but just haven't recognized it yet. For example, I suspect that if you have two or more clients in one particular industry, you're developing a niche. Your challenge is to concentrate on it and cultivate it.

## One Thing at a Time

Famous nineteenth-century English novelist Charles Dickens once wrote, "I never could have done what I have done without the . . . determination to concentrate myself on one subject at a time."

A century or so later, a famous—or rather infamous—American echoed Dickens' message when he said, "Success in any endeavor requires single-minded attention to detail and total concentration."

A common theme, indeed, but spoken by two men who almost certainly had absolutely nothing else in common. The latter was none other than the notorious Willie Sutton, whose "career"—which lasted from the mid-1920s until 1952—entailed a three-decade crime spree. The objects of Sutton's "single-minded attention to detail" were banks, about a hundred in all, from which he made sizable and unauthorized withdrawals of funds—at gunpoint.

After several arrests and many years behind bars, Sutton eventually recognized that he would probably be better off finding a different niche. After his release from prison in 1969, he again turned his single-mindedness to the banking industry; only this time as a consultant, advising bank officials on how to improve their anti-robbery techniques.

By whatever name it's called—single-mindedness, determination, concentration, or specialization—that's what it takes to identify your niche and position yourself successfully in it.

There are countless examples in the history of the U.S. businesses of men and women who've achieved great success because they found the right niche and established it as the foundation for their success. The stories of people like Henry Ford, Mary Kay Ash, Walt Disney, Lance Armstrong, Ray Kroc, and so many others are oft-repeated and well-known.

Kroc, for example, became famous after purchasing a small San Bernardino, California, restaurant owned by brothers Richard and Maurice McDonald—and transforming it into the world's largest fast-food restaurant chain. Early on, the signs in front of the famous Golden Arches would show the running totals on the number of hamburgers sold throughout the McDonald's chain: ("10,000,000 Sold," "50,000,000 Sold," "One Billion Sold," and so on). Eventually, those signs simply read: "Billions and Billions Sold."

There's a little-known story about Ray Kroc that reveals his "single-minded attention to detail" that I heard from a friend and colleague who had a chance meeting with Kroc many years ago. My friend was the president of a Florida bank not far from where the hamburger king was staying. One day, Kroc came into the bank, where he didn't have an account, and asked a bank representative if he could get a check cashed. The banker, quite properly, asked Kroc for identification. After approving the check, the young bank officer asked: "What do you do, Mr. Kroc?"

Instead of taking offense, as some other prominent individuals might have done, or announcing that he was the CEO of McDonald's, Kroc simply replied, "I sell hamburgers." Single-mindedness, indeed!

## The Niche Formation

Ray Kroc clearly knew what his niche was. But what about you? What's your niche? Maybe it's some employees of the same company. Maybe it's a particular industry or a geographic area. It could be situational; for instance, if you're divorced, you have a personal understanding of what that process is like, and you've experienced the way in which money moves when there's a divorce in process. I know of attorneys and financial advisors, for instance, who do perhaps 80 percent of their work with divorcees. They understand that market and get many referrals from divorcees.

Become an expert in a particular situational area. Identify industry influencers. If you conduct detailed targeted marketing and see your referrals increase, you've become the authority in that area.

People like to work with professionals who understand their situation and who are experts in their particular industry or specialty. So if you're not in a niche right now, identify several areas that have potential for you and begin developing ties to them. It's not always easy to become entrenched in a niche, but once you get there, you can really begin to score. A financial advisor client of mine increased his business *by 1,000 percent* in three years, simply by focusing his marketing strategies on that niche. So I have seen, firsthand, how well this works.

There are many other ways to position yourself in a niche. Keep in mind that you don't necessarily have to limit yourself to one. If there are two or more that "are specially suited to your abilities," by all means, get busy and cultivate them.

### Niche to Your Competency

The story of Jim and Naomi Rhode—founders of the Phoenix, Arizona–based marketing company SmartPractice—is a classic case study of the success that can be achieved by concentrating on the right niche.

Early in his career, Jim Rhode used his engineering background to do long-range planning in the corporate world, while Naomi, with a background in dentistry, worked as a dental hygienist and had begun a professional speaking career. In the late 1960s, Jim had been recruited to help get a dental laboratory started.

By then, it had become apparent that their talents—Jim, the practical, analytical left-brained one, and Naomi, right-brained with strong people skills—were different, but at the same time, highly complementary. They worked well together and, in 1972, reports Naomi, "We chose to meld our competencies for success."

The niche they chose was dentistry, an area in which they both had experience. This illustrates what you might describe as the first law of developing a niche—ask yourself, "What do I know?" Naomi said emphatically, *"Niche to your competency."*

The Rhodes use a simple triangle to illustrate the strategies on which SmartPractice has been built. The three points represent product, seminars, and speaking, each functioning synergistically with the other two. Jim explains, "Understanding and respecting the market is so important in building your niche. For example, we knew that one thing dentists need is an effective recall system to enable them to keep in regular contact with their patients, and to remind them when to schedules their next visits. So we developed, designed, and started manufacturing and distributing products aimed at helping dentists communicate more effectively with those patients."

Jim also points out the opportunities that exist to conduct seminars within a niche. "Just about every industry has a national association," he said, "with smaller affiliated groups in each state. That's 52 annual meetings at the state level, plus perhaps three or four nationally—all of which provide multiple opportunities to present educational seminars and workshops."

Jim is careful to point out that seminars may be loss leaders in and of themselves, but they're an excellent way to form and cultivate relationships. The SmartPractice seminars have had a major role in establishing the company's reputation—not only across the United States, but internationally as well.

The third point of the triangle—speaking—has also contributed significantly to the company's success. Both Naomi and Jim Rhode are highly skilled professional speakers who regularly address groups all over the world. Each has served as president of the National Speakers Association, and Naomi is also a past president of the Global Speakers Federation.

As the company grew and flourished, it became clear that its systems and products for dentists were also applicable in other professions, which opened up several new niches. The result has been a customer base which—in addition to more than 125,000 dentists—includes physicians, chiropractors, eye care professionals, and veterinarians. Manufacturing facilities are in the United States and on the Pacific Rim, serving customers here at home, as well as in Canada, Germany, England, Japan, Australia, and New Zealand.

## Getting Started

There are numerous strategies you can use to identify your niche and gain a foothold in it.

### Trade Associations

Join a trade association and become the expert for that industry. Start by going to the library and researching all the associations that are out there. Pick one or two to which you feel you can make a contribution, and attend a few of their meetings. Join one of them to get started and, *voilà*! You've gained access to its membership list and publications. But don't simply join—*get involved*. Your active participation will help you build your niche. Remember: People do business with people they know, like, and—most importantly—trust.

### Publications

Consider writing articles for industry publications. Perhaps you can even produce a targeted industry newsletter or prepare a special report on a currently relevant topic. With the Internet at your fingertips, your ability to conduct research on almost any subject is virtually unlimited.

Anywhere from 50 percent to 80 percent of articles in newspapers and trade journals are generated from press releases and publicity. Trade journals are often on the lookout for well-written articles that focus on areas of interest to their readers. If you submit one or two good ones, the editors may keep coming back to you for more. That kind of exposure quickly positions you as an expert in your field and increases the likelihood of attracting prospective clients.

### Seminars

You can also create educational opportunities to cultivate your niche, like conducting seminars for a particular segment of the marketplace. Small business associations, chambers of commerce, and other organizations host periodic "brown bag" lunches or breakfast meetings, and are often looking for speakers for these events.

Check the calendar section of your local newspaper to see which organizations hold these kinds of programs, and then contact them. You probably won't get any fees, but it's a great way to solidify your position in a particular niche and develop a stream of prospects.

And don't overlook individual companies. Many regularly bring in outsiders to conduct training seminars or educational workshops for their staff members. Do a good job the first time, and you may be invited back often. If you can't get into the company, and it's a union shop, perhaps you can gain entrée through union officials and provide seminars, presentations, or educational workshops for union members.

## Sponsorships

Sponsorships offer excellent opportunities for you to gain significant added exposure for the product or service you provide. Simply consider what you provide—as well as the audience to whom you cater—to come up with ideas for events or products you might subsidize. For example, if you sell health food supplements and vitamin products and your niche is the senior market, finding a sponsorship opportunity should be relatively easy.

You may have to get really creative here to find the right combination. If the employees of a large company in your marketplace are your niche, find out what activities and events that company hosts for its employees, and sponsor one or more of them. If product donation isn't a good fit, consider other opportunities, such as funding the company's bowling or softball team, or underwriting its newsletter's production costs.

In the words of Walt Kelly's cartoon character Pogo, "We're surrounded by insurmountable opportunities." Pick out a couple, and go ahead and surmount them!

## Your Client Base

There's certainly no better way to hone a niche than to enlist the help of the clients you already have in that niche. If you've developed a solid relationship with your clients and they trust you, all you have to do is ask for their help. In most cases, they'll gladly take your materials and spread the word about you to their colleagues and friends.

> What's your niche market?
>
> _____
> _____
> _____
> _____

## Beware the Naysayers

Many useful, virtually indispensable products we take for granted today might never have come into being if the pessimists had been calling the shots. These include the telephone, the radio, moving pictures with sound, and the computer. In 1876, for example, an internal Western Union memo stated, "This 'telephone' has too many shortcomings to be seriously considered as a means of communication. The device is inherently of no value to us." In 1927, cofounder of Warner Brothers Movie Studios Harry M. Warner asked, "Who the hell wants to hear actors talk?" And the advent of the computer was greeted with skepticism by many naysayers. Thomas J. Watson Sr., president of IBM for more than 40 years, was widely reported to have said, "I think there is a world market for maybe five computers"; but it's more likely that it came from another source within IBM.

Still, in 1949, _Popular Mechanics_ magazine reported that, "computers in the future may have only 1,000 vacuum tubes and perhaps weigh no more than 1.5 tons." And, in 1957, a Prentice Hall editor wrote, "I can assure you that data processing is a fad that won't last out the year."

As recently as 1977, a practical use for computers was still being debunked in some quarters. That year, no less an "expert" than Ken Olson—who had cofounded Digital Equipment Corporation 20 years earlier—told attendees at a meeting of the World Future Society, "There is no reason for any individual to have a computer in his home."

## Find Your "Natural Niche" . . . And Never Let It Go

Remember: You can't be all things to all people, and you shouldn't try to be. Taking into account your expertise, areas of interest, and the niche areas in which you're already working, decide what kind of "specialist" you want to be. It should feel natural, as if you were born to play this role.

Ask yourself, "Who are the people I _really_ like to do business with?" Analyze your current client base by writing down specific names and the business these people are in. Ask yourself what the plusses and minuses are for you in each case. Once you've finished your analysis, a pretty clear picture of your "natural niche" should emerge.

*Then, cultivate that niche! For example:*

✓ Target the top two publications in your industry and write dynamite articles for them. Make this a priority! If writing isn't one of your strengths, hire a pro to write some articles for you.

✓ Become a prominent and visible member of the best trade association in your industry.

✓ Create educational opportunities, such as seminars and workshops. Be innovative! You'll make a name for yourself as an expert in your field.

✓ Use testimonials and success stories in your particular niche; they act like referrals, and can go a long way in helping you build your nest.

---

### Take 15 and Get Your Clients Going Wild! *A 15-Minute Client-Builder Exercise*

List a niche you will focus on and your focused activities within that niche.

_____

_____

_____

_____

---

## In Other Words

*I cannot give you the formula for success, but I can give you the formula for failure, which is—try to please everybody.*

*—Herbert Bayard Swope*

CHAPTER

10

# Techniques for Creating a Memorable Experience

## Give 'Em Something to Talk About!

*Creating loyalty among clients is directly fostered by the memorable experience you create.*

### The Age of Experience

It's really a whole new world out there. Today, the way to truly rise above the competition, delight your customers, receive stellar ratings, and protect your client base is to create an experience for them. You don't want to be or become a commodity—something that's capable of being interchanged or replaced. Even service-based businesses today fear—and are—becoming "commoditized"; they can't be differentiated from one another, and their prices are solely determined by market demand. You want to provide something different for your customers: *an experience that's created by how you make them feel.*

And even if you already know about creating experiences, the question is: Have you created an experience? *Really?* The first step in delivering an experience is determining what your differentiation is—and keep in mind that it may just be *you.*

What is your differentiation? In other words—what distinguishes you from your competition, from other companies and/or people who offer similar products and services?

_____

_____

_____

_____

## Many Experiences Are Well-Planned

Think of some memorable experiences you've enjoyed, perhaps at a theme park, a unique restaurant, or some other kind of event. These didn't take place by accident; chances are that someone (or several people) carefully planned the details of each one. The companies involved intentionally and thoroughly designed the experience they wanted their clients to have.

Consider something as seemingly simple as a visit to a bookstore. Once upon a time, about all bookstores included were rows of bookshelves and a cash register. You went in, found the books you wanted, paid, and left. They were basically in the commodity business. Not anymore! Today's bookstore features comfortable furniture where you can sit and read to your heart's content. You can also find a wide array of magazines, local and out-of-town newspapers, sections with CDs and DVDs, the occasional book club gathering, an area where you can buy or trade used books, and, of course, a refreshment area where you can enjoy an almost limitless variety of coffee products or soft drinks, bagels, doughnuts, sandwiches, and cookies. Bookstores have actually become a place to socialize.

On a recent visit to one of the large chain bookstores, I found nearly all of the above—plus gifts, greeting cards, puzzles, games, stationery, calendars, music CDs, fine chocolates, and more. And for shoppers who actually wanted to look at some books but had left their glasses at home, the store also sold—you guessed it—reading glasses! While there, I received a copy of the store newsletter and an application to join its frequent-buyer club from one of the employees. One store official told me the chain does $15 million a year in sales—of *chocolates*! And it sells more coffee to its customers than all but the largest coffee outlets. Everything in the store says, "Come in and stay for a while; relax and enjoy your visit." It's no longer a matter of simply buying a book or two; it's been transformed into an *experience*.

## How Are You Creating Your Experience?

Think about how you personally create an experience. For example, I have one client who is health-conscious. This client wants everyone around him to live healthier, more active lives, so he incorporates nutritious food and informational videos, books, posters, and seminars into his unrelated business offerings. He's providing an experience: a complete "healthy life" plan that focuses on his clients' overall well-being, and allows him to connect with people on a different level.

Another long-time client of mine provides postcards featuring unique aspects of his office to his valued clients as they're finishing up their appointments. The clients are asked to jot a quick note to a friend or associate and address the postcard, which my client then stamps and mails. It's akin to going on vacation; you want to share the experience with your friends, so you send a postcard. The same could be done by printing buttons or T-shirts with the name of your business and the experience on it.

Yet another one of my clients has created "The Life Enjoyment Experience®"—the idea being that he helps his clients "get to the top of the mountain." And from the mountaintop, you can see and experience the world. Therefore, he has decorated each office and conference room in his headquarters to represent a different part of the world. Each room has a huge mural of a city on the wall and a collection of items from that place. He has a London room, Washington, DC room, Venice room, and so forth. He reports that people bring their friends by to see his unique facilities, even without an appointment. Can you imagine a better way to attract new business?

That's one of the great things about experiences: people who have positive ones want to share them with others. And, even in today's economy, clients will pay a premium for an experience.

### Give Them Something to Talk About

Bonnie Raitt sings in her hit song "Something to Talk About" that people are going to talk anyway, so let's *really* give them something to talk about. In business, however, people may not ever talk about you unless you give them a good reason to do so. What would cause your clients to want to remember the experience they had at your business? What is it that sets you apart from and above your competition? Have you given them something good to talk about?

What aspects of your business do people want to talk about?

_____

_____

_____

_____

## Marketing to Current Clients Creates a Tangible Experience

Despite all these facts, many business and professional people still believe that they must go out and "market to" cold prospects to increase their revenues. They explain it by claiming that, "That's just the way it's always been done." But marketing to your existing clients really *works*, and I'm going to demonstrate that through the following examples.

The first time I witnessed dramatic results from client marketing took place while I was working with a financial advisor and his firm who hired me to help him improve his marketing strategies and bring on new clients. The principle in the firm measured progress by the amount of client assets brought under its management at the firm. His goal was to grow into a large financial services firm with hundreds of millions in money under management.

Since I had not worked with a financial services firm prior to this (thanks to this client, I now work with hundreds of financial firms each year!), I started by looking at the opportunities that existed, and the type of prospecting that may work for attracting clients who would invest their savings with this firm. I asked this financial advisor how he had acquired clients in the past. He informed me that much of his success was rooted in his fear of prospecting. He didn't want to cold call or employ similar strategies, so he just kept calling and talking with those who had already done business with his firm. He kept himself busy by avoiding the typical prospecting strategies of reaching people who didn't know him.

The result was unintentional but amazing: his handful of clients *truly* loved him. They cared about his success, brought him food, and even sent birthday cards to his wife and his growing family. And a valuable by-product of this was a stream of referrals. This advisor had little experience—he was only in his twenties at the time. Yet his drive and determination to stay in business and communicate properly with his few clients prompted them to genuinely like and trust him. As a result, they began recommending him to others who worked at the same company.

I knew that attempting to garner business from people with whom he had no connection was going to be a long shot for this advisor, based on his lack of propensity for prospecting. So, I simply took his model of communicating and acquiring referrals and made a system out of it. The experience he was delivering was his connection with others; he just needed to do it more systematically and with a larger number of people. And his staff needed to do the same.

Today, this firm is one of the top financial firms in the United States, managing hundreds of millions in client assets.

Is it possible to build an entire multimillion-dollar business around the ability to create an experience based on one person's capacity to connect with others? It certainly seems so. And it is the best way to build a business effectively, efficiently, profitably, and quickly.

Others firms have seen the kind of success that this advisor and his firm have enjoyed. I have been asked to do just what did in his firm: build a model around the acquisition of referrals. I have developed the following five-point system for doing so:

1. *Delight clients* through a total of 12 personal interactions per year—both calls and one-on-one meetings.

2. *Acquire referrals*, which just seem to come when you have personal contact with people in combination with delivery of quality products or services.

3. *Invite referrals to educational workshops*. Engage your prospects/referrals through a soft introduction to the firm. This could be done online through a short video, as well. See Chapter 15, "Traditional Marketing Still Works."

4. *Acquire clients*. After a referral has attended a live workshop, there is more than an 80 percent chance that this person will schedule a one-on-one meeting, and then the sales process begins.

5. *Repeat process* from #1.

It is actually a straightforward strategy. It simply requires that you systematize your operation around delighting your customers, building niches of clients, providing educational workshops, converting clients, and then repeating the entire process from the beginning. I have employed this system with great success in many firms. However, as you may imagine, it is not as easily executed as it may appear to be. The key is the very first step: to delight clients. How you manage to do this, however, is much more complex than just sending them a few letters and visiting with them once a year to go over their accounts. It is a process that begins with the learned and cultivated ability to connect and create a memorable experience.

## Keeping in Touch

You want to plan to "wow" your clients right from the start by introducing a program of proactive personal communications that will surprise and please them. In today's world, the more frequently you contact them, the better the relationship is likely to be.

Do your best clients contact you, or do you contact them more frequently? Who initiates interactions between the two of you? If your best clients are always forced to begin communication with you, the less satisfied they're likely to be.

You need to make sure that there is always a "next activity" scheduled in your database for important clients. This is the easiest way to remind yourself to contact the person, and it will ensure that he or she doesn't fall through the cracks. You could give the clients a call, invite them to lunch, e-mail them, or simply drop a note in the mail. Plan your next contact or appointment with a client during your current one; it is a sure-fire way of maintaining consistency and implementation.

If you are wondering how many times you should be contacting people, begin by setting your floor—not ceiling—of possible contacts you can make in a week, and work from there. The goal should be a consistent number of links. The following are some scheduled activities to put in your database.

- Schedule a phone appointment.
- Make a proactive phone call.
- E-mail a client whenever you come across anything that might be of interest to that person.
- Invite clients to educational workshops.
- Invite clients to lunch or other social meetings.
- Invite clients to a meeting in your office.
- Mail a personal note.

Even if you have a large network, you can still break it down to a manageable number and reach out to specific people individually.

*List your 20 best clients*

1. _____

2. _____

3. _____

4. _____

5. _____

6. _____

7. _____

8. _____

9. _____

10. _____

11. _____

12. _____

13. _____

14. _____

15. _____

16. _____

17. _____

18. _____

19. _____

20. _____

How do you regularly keep in touch with each of the people or companies listed above? List the various media you use, and how often you use each one.

_____

_____

_____

_____

## Set Yourself Apart

Realtors are an example of one profession where there are hundreds of competitors in a single, local area—all have identical fees and access to the same inventory. However, I know of a Realtor in one of the nation's fastest-growing counties who found a way to become the first one most people in the area call when they're ready to put their home on the market. He does all the same activities that other Realtors do, including putting up signs, running ads, holding open houses, and showing properties; but that's not what sets him apart. Unlike his competitors, he doesn't just show up when someone wants to buy or sell a house. Each spring, every homeowner in the area gets a tiny tree from him to replant in his or her yard; in October, a pumpkin accompanied by a note from him appears on each front porch. In mid-summer, his antique fire engine, loaded with neighborhood kids, is at the head of the local Independence Day parade. He's consistently the top Realtor in his area in good times and even in the more difficult times I have seen. He does what his competitors don't do—he creates experiences!

## Video and Audio on Your Web Site

Your media and communication channels can also be used to create encounters with clients. You can provide a link on your web site to video or audio podcasts that include a few minutes of interesting information about the business, industry, or clients. You can then inform clients through a link in an e-mail of the video update on your site. When you are the one who is speaking to customers, you provide more personal communication—especially if it's regularly updated—than simply writing something on your site. You can e-mail your video with a personal message through a relatively new service called www .AdvisorTLC.com, which creates a *very* unique and memorable experience for your clients.

Founder of the business development consulting firm Sittig Incorporated and author of three books on "The Blitz Experience" of prospecting and business expansion Andrea Sittig-Rolf has discovered valuable ways to keep in touch with her Fortune 100 clients. "I prepare monthly video tips with valuable information for those that have opted in," Sittig-Rolf explains. She is staying in front of her largest clients regularly by providing them with information that she is personally delivering.

## Conference Call or Webinar

You can host regular conference calls or webinars on interesting information as a good way to personally stay in touch, because *you* are the one presenting the message. You can use free services and record the calls for later broadcast at www.FreeConferenceCall.com. A financial advisor in Ohio records a monthly call on the state of the market with his commentary. He also includes a few "fun facts," as he calls them, on things unrelated to financial services. Many businesses send e-mail or printed newsletters—this advisor has given his information a much more personal touch. He notes that clients use it as a referral tool by directing people to his recordings as a way of sharing his expertise with others.

## Unique Events that Go "The Extra Mile"

Hosting a memorable event to which you invite clients and prospects can help build and deepen relationships, and create a lasting memory of a terrific experience. In the highly competitive public relations (PR) and communications industries, a company needs to be memorable to succeed. Strauss Radio Strategies, Inc., in Washington, DC has found that going the extra mile in client relationships always pays off. The company is widely regarded by both the PR industry and political insiders as an expert on radio public relations and political communication on the radio. "This 'extra mile' can take many forms," said founder Richard Strauss. "I never hesitate to show a client how much they are appreciated."

Last year, for instance, the firm organized an ice-cream social for TMG Strategies, a client of 13 years. They had worked on many projects for TMG's Fortune 100 clients, and wanted to show the firm and its president, Dan McGinn, how much they valued the business in a positive and memorable way. So in October 2008, they invited the entire TMG staff to a special ice-cream social. The idea behind this occasion was to breathe new life into a long-standing client relationship. By spearheading a fun event for both companies to enjoy, everyone involved was reminded of *why* they worked together—and how much they both benefit from the partnership.

"We greeted everyone personally at the door at the event, welcoming old colleagues and meeting many new ones. My staff and I even helped serve banana splits from behind a full-feature ice cream bar!" Strauss said. "Later on, I invited Dan to give a short presentation, which turned out to be a great opportunity for Strauss Radio and TMG to look back on our past projects and mutual accomplishments."

The event was a great success, and it was *certainly* memorable. Dozens of pictures were taken and were later compiled into photo booklets for McGinn and his coworkers.

"Many of the TMG staffers told me they were touched, and they still bring up the event from time to time," Strauss said. "We ended 2008 on a positive note, giving TMG momentum to continue working with us in the New Year."

By going the extra mile, Strauss Radio Strategies solidified a client relationship of 13 years that will surely continue to grow.

## What Are the Consequences of Not Creating an Experience?

Dissatisfied clients not only go elsewhere, they also tell others of their dissatisfaction with your organization. And, in most cases, they won't even tell you they're dissatisfied. In fact, for each client that *does* complain to you, there are nine others who'll just disappear without bothering to tell you why. What's even worse is that those 10 disappointed clients will each tell an average of five other people about their displeasure with you. That means that every complaint you receive represents up to 60 people who are walking around with a negative image of your company—and talking about it! I call it "The Rule of 60," something that definitely doesn't belong in your game plan.

This is also where the 80/20 rule comes into play—a maxim that states that most businesses get 80 percent of their revenue from 20 percent of their existing client base. Typically, however, these same businesses spend 60 percent to 80 percent of their marketing dollars communicating with noncustomers and people who may never end up doing business with the firm. You should instead focus 80 percent of your efforts on clients, and 20 percent on prospects. Otherwise, you're likely to face situations where those 20 percent of your clients who bring in 80 percent of your revenue are unhappy and telling others—primarily because you're spending your marketing dollars and efforts in the wrong places.

### The Cheesehead Phenomenon

Sometimes you do things in certain circumstances that you normally wouldn't do—because of the experience you're undergoing or the company you're keeping. For example, I am a dedicated Green Bay Packer fan, born and raised in Wisconsin. You may have noticed that many Packer fans wear on their heads what is commonly referred to as a "cheesehead." Now, really, what would possess someone of seemingly normal intelligence to wear a cheesehead? Would these fans wear their cheeseheads to the bank or grocery store? I hope not! But they would—and *do*—wear the yellow foam hat in public, at games, and actually *try* to be on TV in front of millions of people! The reason behind this fanatic behavior is what I call the "Cheesehead Phenomenon"—something that occurs when the experience of which you are a part causes you to do something you wouldn't otherwise do.

The Packer enthusiasm comes from generations of adoring fans who have backed the team through many years of losing, in the same way they have supported them through years of winning. Loyal fans do just that. Packer fans have a great desire to be a part of the experience of going to a game at Lambeau Field. They outwardly show their pride for their team and the state of Wisconsin, starting with a non-negotiable necessity of creating or attending a pregame tailgate party filled with lots of brats, beer, and cheese. Fans wear all sorts of cheesehead gear and other unique hunting clothing (some of the warmest clothing you can get for northern weather). People are there for the game, to see their beloved team win, and for the fun as well. They show up when the team has a losing record, merely for the connection with like-minded people and for the thrill that the thought of winning brings. Attending a game at Lambeau Field is truly an experience. And for that, some do something they wouldn't normally do—they wear cheeseheads to show off their "fandemonium."

This is akin to when your clients go out of their way to help you, refer business to you, or drop you a note of thanks—something they otherwise ordinarily would not do. Because most people think about themselves and their own lives, your goal should be to deliver your service or product in a unique way that touches them personally. If you can get people to think about you for a little bit longer, everyone wins!

---

How do you want your clients to show their "love" for your business?

_____

_____

_____

_____

---

## Tell Them What *You* Do

In some cases—more often than you may think—you are providing an experience for your clients that they don't recognize or even know about.

So find ways to create tangible reminders of the intangible service your clients may have received.

For example, do you update your clients systematically on progress as you are working with them? Sometimes you can get so involved in back-end and behind-the-scenes work that your client doesn't know what's going on, or worse—assumes that nothing is happening. You have to inform your clients about what you've been doing on their behalf in order for them to recognize and appreciate your efforts.

Another way of showing what you do is by creating something called a "Deliverables Document"—something that explains in detail exactly what you did for the client when you finish a project with him or her. For instance, if on completion of the project your web designer gave you a document that detailed the purpose of the web site in layman's terms, how all the pieces fit together, and an "access" page that listed any user-name/passwords associated with the account (ftp, blog, and so on)— wouldn't that be valuable? And it wouldn't be expected.

---

## Take 15 and Get Your Clients Going Wild!
### *A 15-Minute Client-Builder Exercise*

What are possible deliverable documents you could create? Think of some projects you've recently done for clients, and be as specific as you can.

_____

_____

_____

_____

What are the experiences you will create for your clients?

_____

_____

_____

_____

# Your Best Prospects Come from Referrals

## Scripts and Strategies for Increasing Your Introductions to Others

*People will never talk about you to others if you haven't given them something unique or different to say.*

Positive word of mouth is one of the most coveted outcomes of great products and service. It is also perhaps the best thing that can happen to any business. A good reputation generates referrals—which are often the most profitable leads that a business can receive. Clients who you acquire through referrals are more loyal, easier to close, more cost-efficient, and in turn are often the ones to give you even *more* referrals.

Consumers today trust a personal recommendation more than traditional advertising, a brochure, a web site, or other company communications. According to the Word of Mouth Marketing Association (WOMMA), two-thirds of all economic activity in the United States is influenced by shared opinions about a product, brand, or service. Yet according to eMarketer—a leading web site on digital marketing and media research and analysis—only 18 percent of businesses have a referral program in place.

Most of you inherently understand the benefits of having your clients refer their friends, family, and colleagues, but you simply fail to actively make it part of your marketing plan—and realize that earning and acquiring referrals requires a systematic approach. But before you can create and implement a referral system, it is first helpful to determine what may currently be limiting referrals to your business.

## The Reasons You May Not Get the Referrals You Want

Most businesspeople would probably agree that they would like to get more referrals or recommendations and have more raving fans. Some critical questions that you must ask yourself when considering why you might *not* be receiving more referrals are:

- Are you *truly* referable—or could you be more so?
- Are you doing what you said you would? (Sometimes that's not nearly enough.)

Let's look at each question individually.

### Are You Truly Referable?

Good businesspeople, businesses, and brands are referable—for the most part. If you were to ask all of your current clients if they would ever refer business to you, *most* would respond positively. On average, 80 percent of a healthy business's clients claim that they *would* give you a referral. So . . . why don't they?

Because it is human nature to consciously or subconsciously consider the potential things that could go wrong when providing a referral or recommendation to another person. In contemplating whether to refer a friend, colleague, or family member to another professional, you tend to ask questions like, will it work out? Will it make you look bad? Will something go wrong? If there is even the slightest inkling that this might not go well, referrals will not come.

However, if you truly believe that you are delighting your clients and still are not receiving regular referrals from them, it's possible that there may be a discrepancy in viewpoints. An insider's perception of the business is not necessarily the same as a client's view. And although it doesn't mean that you must be doing something wrong, it's certainly worth checking out.

One way to find this out for sure is to conduct a "Client Delight Survey" that you can mail or e-mail; or you can use an online survey service like www.surveymonkey.com to give your clients an easy opportunity to provide you with feedback. It's easy to design your survey online and send a link to your clients for access. You can then view your results as they are collected in real time—including live graphs and charts, as well as individual responses. There are also functions that allow you to download a summary of your results. You can also download all the raw data and export it to a spreadsheet for further analysis.

A typical survey can be set up in the following way, where you ask participants to note whether (and to what degree) they agree or disagree with statements such as:

- Our organization is totally committed to the idea of keeping you informed and satisfied.

- Rather than having to undo mistakes, we seem to "do things right the first time."

- Our organization appears to be totally committed to the idea of quality.

- We regularly provide valuable information to you.

- We maintain adequate contact with you.

- We make it easy for you to do business with us.

- Our employees often go above and beyond to serve you well. This is a good opportunity to ask customers to list specific employees.

- We sincerely try to resolve all your complaints.

- We make it easy for you to contact us.

- Our employees seem to have a good understanding of all our products and services.

- I would be willing to recommend someone to you.

## Are You Doing What You Said You Would?

If yes, this may be the real reason clients don't refer you as often as they should. Simply put, you're not getting the referrals you deserve because you are doing *exactly* what you said you would do. Although there is nothing wrong with that, it is not unique or exciting, and it won't cause people to talk about you or your company. Your clients will talk when there is something to say—something unexpected that stands out from the competition. They talk about you when you do something that was (pleasantly, of course!) surprising to them. Doing exactly what you said you would do and nothing more makes you a good person and businessperson, but it isn't very exciting. To get your clients to share you with the world, you need to do or say something that gets them to say or think, *wow* (see Chapter 10, "Techniques for Creating a Memorable Experience").

So try sending your clients a handwritten note and coupon; e-mail them a personal video you just recorded; call and wish them a Happy Birthday; or send a weekly e-zine to stay in touch. Give them more than they expected and you will get just what you deserve—more referrals than you've ever had before.

## Acquiring a Stream of Qualified Referrals Needs a System

If you provide valuable, worthwhile products and services to your clients, then they'll want to share you with others—it's just human nature! Sometimes they need a little nudge, though. So whatever your business is, you should have a system in place to maintain a steady flow of referral business. Pick a strategy for receiving referrals, and then do it again and again. There's a place to record and plan your strategy at the end of this chapter.

### Just Ask!

The best and most systematic method for acquiring referrals is to simply ask. That's it—just ask! And ask all the time. Use specific wording to share with those people who may be in a position to refer business to you, and tell them exactly the kinds of prospects you want and what products or services you can deliver. Start by creating a "Who We Serve" list of the types of people who are good clients for you, their needs, and how you can help them. Show this list to clients. It is an effective way to get clients to think of qualified people to refer to you, instead of giving the typical response: "I don't know anyone."

Here's an example of this kind of a list:

---

## Who We Serve

| Client Type | Need | Solution |
|---|---|---|
| _____ | _____ | _____ |
| _____ | _____ | _____ |
| _____ | _____ | _____ |
| _____ | _____ | _____ |

---

## Tell the Truth—The Whole Truth—Nothing But the Truth

One approach to obtaining referrals is to simply be honest and sincere with your clients and ask them for their help. It's basic human nature for people to generally respond much more positively to a request for help than they will to being pressured. And when do you ask for referrals? *Every single time* you're in touch with your clients—by using the following approaches.

### Ask Open-Ended Questions

- "What have you liked about the work we've done together?"

- Mention the benefits you've provided to them and then ask, "Wouldn't you agree?" When you get a positive response, simply follow up by asking, "Is there anyone else you know who may need our services? If so, I'd be grateful if you'd send them my way. Or, if you'll give me their names, I'll be happy to contact them."

- Tell them, "My expertise is working with people like you who have a need for the [products, services, etc.] I provide. Who else do you know who may need my help?"

- Ask, "Do you know anyone who is nervous about [insert the fear your product solves] their retirement/affording homeowners insurance/cost of college/finding a job?"

## Getting Others to Ask for Referrals

Asking works better sometimes when *you* aren't the one doing the asking; success in asking for referrals often begins with *who* is asking, and is often better received when done by staff members. These people have credibility with customers because generally a staff person doesn't own the company and therefore is not trying to sell someone something for his or her own personal gain. An employee won't likely benefit directly by asking a client for a referral. In general, people don't give their word about something unless they are benefiting—or they *truly* believe in it! If a staff person talks, for instance, about how their boss is such a diligent, hard-working, and caring financial advisor—it carries credibility because it is different. Do your employees tell clients what they think of you—in a good way? Do they ask for referrals? Because if they did—I bet you'd get many more than you're getting now.

## Sample Referral Script for Staff

> *I know Michael really truly appreciates working with you and helping with your legal needs. I've seen him help clients through some very difficult times, especially recently; and we've been getting a lot of referrals from our clients because of it. I know Michael wants to help as many people as he can that need quality legal counsel. Let us know if there is anyone else who you think might benefit from the same services that you have received. Let me know and I can have them talk to Michael; if anything, just to ease their mind.*

# Create a Referral Event to Get Clients Talking

"Don't Miss the Boat" is an extremely successful event strategy for giving clients a reason to immediately give you referrals. It is similar to a client appreciation event, but the only people invited are those clients that have referred others to your business. A financial services firm in Detroit was the first to host an event like this—which resulted in more than 40 referrals. Since then, similar success stories have been duplicated across the country by businesses of all types.

## Sample Script to Introduce the Event

> *Mr. Client, don't miss the boat! We're holding this not-to-be-missed event on October 15, on the Detroit Star, the dinner boat on the Detroit River. This gala event with music and dinner and dancing is the perfect excuse for you and your wife to get all dressed up for a night out! But, don't miss the boat, because the only people we're inviting are those who have referred clients to us by [event date].*

This event gives customers an immediate incentive to think of someone to whom they can recommend your services. Yes, it may be a little gimmicky, but I have *never* seen this strategy fail. It has consistently produced qualified referrals of 40 or more per event.

In this chapter you find a sample timeline for a "Don't Miss the Boat" event, as well as a sample letter that introduces the event to your clients.

> *Go to www.AndtheClientsWentWild.com to access all of the materials in the "Don't Miss the Boat" event campaign. Enter the code: WILD to download the materials for free! See Figure 11.1.*

| Time prior to event | Activity | √ | Completion Date |
|---|---|---|---|
| 12–4 months | Reserve event facility, entertainment, caterer | ☐ | __/__/__ |
| 4 months | Mail DMTB program intro letter to top clients | ☐ | __/__/__ |
| 3 months | Mail DMTB invite postcard to all clients | ☐ | __/__/__ |
| 3 months | E-mail electronic version of invitation to all clients | ☐ | __/__/__ |
| 3 months | Promote DMTB event and details on web site | ☐ | __/__/__ |
| 3 months | Post extra postcards within office (i.e., at reception desk) | ☐ | __/__/__ |
| 3 months | Provide postcard to clients in regular meetings | ☐ | __/__/__ |
| 3 months | Include postcard with all other client mailings | ☐ | __/__/__ |
| 2 months | Mail follow-up letter and/or postcard to all clients | ☐ | __/__/__ |
| 2 months | E-mail follow-up e-invitation to all clients | ☐ | __/__/__ |
| 1 month | Reconfirm event facility, entertainment, caterer | ☐ | __/__/__ |
| 1 month thru event date | Mail confirmation letter to all qualifiers requesting RSVP | ☐ | __/__/__ |
| 1 week | Call any registered clients that have not RSVP'd | ☐ | __/__/__ |
| 3 days | Confirm count w/facility and caterer | ☐ | __/__/__ |
| 3 days | Prepare any event materials (ex: Thank You speech) | ☐ | __/__/__ |

*Source*: Redzone Marketing, Inc.

**Example of letter:**
Date
NAME
ADDRESS
CITY, STATE ZIP
Dear NAME,

PICTURE OF BOAT

# Don't Miss the Boat!

On MONTH ___, 20___ at ___ PM we are hosting the First Annual **COMPANY NAME** *Referral Celebration Cruise* filled with dinner, dancing, and fun down the _____ River.

This inaugural trip is part of a new program at COMPANY NAME. We are **Celebrating** all of the referrals that we receive into our business. This event is our way of saying Thank You to all of our clients and associates who have referred business to us in [YEAR]. We consider it an honor and a privilege to receive your referrals. Our business has grown tremendously and much of that is due to recommendations we receive from clients like you.

**Admission:** FREE for anyone who has referred business to us. Our thanks to you!

If you know of anyone who has the need for a _____ or would like to get a second opinion on their current _____, please refer them to COMPANY NAME. We will ensure that they will receive the same high-quality counsel and services that you receive, and we'll meet without charge or obligation.

Attached, please find a form that you can fill out. Thank you for your referrals and we look forward to seeing you on the [boat name] in MONTH!
Sincerely,
NAME

## REFERRALS

**Please use this form to share with us those you would like to introduce to the firm. Thank you!**

REFERRED BY: _____

Name _____

Address _____

City _____ State _____ Zip Code
_____

Home Phone _____ Work Phone _____

Best Time to Contact _____

*(continued)*

(*continued*)

---

*Please Check One*

_____ **YES**, please contact the above referral, as we have already talked to them, and they are expecting your call! Feel free to use our name when you call.

_____ **NO**, we have not talked to the above referral, but feel free to use our name when you call.

. . . . . . . . . . . . . . . . . . . . . . . . . . . . . . . . . . . . . . . . . . . . . . . . . . . .

**Name** _____

**Address** _____

**City** _____ **State** _____ **Zip Code** _____

**Home Phone** _____ **Work Phone** _____

**Best Time to Contact** _____

*Please Check One*

_____ **YES**, please contact the above referral, as we have already talked to them, and they are expecting your call! Feel free to use our name when you call.

_____ **NO**, we have not talked to the above referral, but feel free to use our name when you call.

---

**Figure 11.1   Don't Miss the Boat Campaign**

*Download the "Don't Miss the Boat" campaign free at www.AndtheClientsWentWild.com. Enter the code WILD.

## Create a Free Reward Campaign

Driving more customers through referrals can be done easily through a coordinated campaign. Here are two simple steps to keep the referrals coming:

1. E-mail or mail your customers *special offers* designed to forward or pass along to friends and associates.

2. *Reward* your customers for each successful referral.

A dental practice in Missouri wanted patients to refer friends who needed a new dentist. A letter and e-mail was sent out to existing patients letting them know they could receive a *free* dental cleaning by referring friends who came in for services. Patients received both an electronic and hard copy of a mailed coupon that they would forward to their friends for 50 percent off a dental cleaning. The referral had to be a new patient. When new patients redeemed their coupons (with the name of the person who referred them written on it), the referring patient would receive a thank you e-mail letting him or her know that he or she was credited for a free dental cleaning on the account.

This particular campaign resulted in an increase of more than 400 percent in referrals, and a 17 percent increase in profits in a one-year time period. Another interesting thing happened. The business's regular advertising—newspaper ads and mailers—began to produce more results even though nothing changed about the ad's copy or placements. Because their general exposure had increased, it had prospective patients more excited than ever to try out this new dentist.

## Become a "List Lord"

An association, industry, department, or club membership list can open the door to referrals. For example, if you're having lunch with a member of the local Chamber of Commerce, just pull out the membership list and say, "I was wondering if you know any other members who may be interested in the services I offer?" You'll be pleasantly surprised by the response you get.

The list method works because people want to show that they have influence in the groups to which they belong. Once you have referrals, then you can call these people and say, "Hello, I'm Betty Jones. Bill Smith, a fellow member of the Chamber of Commerce, gave me your name and said you may be interested in the services that I offer. I'd love to buy you lunch." It's a great way to get more referrals without putting anyone on the spot.

## Remember the "R" Word

Put a big sign in your office with a big "R" on it. It's simply a way to help your coworkers, clients, and yourself to create a referral mind-set. You'll know that it means, "Remember Referrals." It may also inspire clients (or even prospects!) to ask about the meaning, which creates the perfect opportunity for you to explain that referrals are the heart of your business, and that you'd appreciate their help. When you're not in your office, a lapel button with an "R" on it will probably generate the same question and increase your opportunities to ask for referrals. Corny? Yes, but memorable and successful, too.

Include the word "Referrals" on agendas you bring to every client/prospect meeting you have so that you won't forget this critical task. Colleagues and staff should all agree to remind each other of the importance of the "R" word. This way, remembering referrals will quickly become an office-wide habit.

## Persuade Your Clients with a Club

No, I'm not suggesting any form of violence; I'm talking about launching a referral club that will create a sense of belonging and encourage members to provide—you guessed it—referrals. You might consider partnering with a local business—Sally's Floral Shop, for example. When the referral-rewards club card is taken to Sally's, she will give the shopper a 10 percent discount on any purchase. Or, perhaps you can send club members a special mailing or newsletter. But whatever type of club you decide to form, be sure that it enhances your company's image and promotes ongoing dialogue with your client. It has to be a two-way street.

## Fuel Your Referrals by Showing Appreciation

The method you use to say thank you to clients who refer can actually perpetuate *more* referrals. If you send a small gift that the referrer uses *right away*, it will prompt those same clients to give more referrals. For example, if you send a $20 fuel card as a referral thank you—when do you think clients will use it? Immediately! And who do you think they'll be thinking of when they use it? You! Most of your good clients want to recommend you to others; they just might need a friendly reminder. This fuel card provides them with an instant, tangible reminder of the service you provide.

Another substantial way to express your appreciation is to sit down with a client for an hour or so to help her grow her business. You might make a donation to her favorite charity, or offer to sponsor her child's Little League team. Be creative—just be sure that you go above and beyond the call of duty to say "thank you" for providing such a valuable and generous service.

## Don't Rule Out Prospects and Family Members as Incredible Referral Sources

Yes—as surprising as it sounds, it is possible to get referrals from competitors, current prospects, and even former prospects. Let's say you've provided valuable information to others who, for whatever reason, decided not to do business with you but still appreciate what you did for them. Why wouldn't they refer business to you?

Other potential referral sources are members of churches, associations, or special interest groups. And don't assume that your family members and friends know exactly what you do. (I can't tell you how many times I've heard from my loved ones, "Now, what is it that you do again?") Your closest relatives are probably your biggest fans, and can be wonderful referral sources, so make sure you have clearly communicated to them what you do for a living.

---

## Take 15 and Get Your Clients Going Wild!
### A 15-Minute Client-Builder Exercise

*What's your referral strategy?*
*Who are your best referral sources?*

Clients? _____

_____

Prospects? _____

_____

Employees? _____

_____

Colleagues? _____

_____

Family and Friends? _____

_____

Vendors? _____

_____

Business and Professional Associations? _____

_____

Social Contacts? _____

_____

Competitors? _____

_____

**How will you thank those who give referrals?**

Letters? _____

_____

E-mail? _____

_____

*(continued)*

*(continued)*

Free services? _____

_____

Events? _____

_____

Coupons? _____

_____

# My Web Site Is Working!

## Turn a Bland Site and Your Internet Presence into a Moneymaker

### Your Online Presence Defines You

When prospects or clients search for you and arrive at your web site, do they see what they want to see? Does the content you provide answer their questions and/or exceed their expectations? Most importantly—does it create a connection between the visitor and your firm?

Recent statistics indicate that people form an opinion of a web site in seven seconds, and will decide within that time frame whether to browse within your site—or move on. With this in mind, it is important to have a web site design that downloads quickly, is aesthetically pleasing, and tells users right away what's in it for them. Simply put, your site needs to stop visitors in their tracks.

Your home page specifically needs to attract attention. This is most effective if the site has a clearly stated message specifically for your target market. If you work with clients who are near or at retirement, have boxes they can click on with phrases like, "Important Information to Know Before You Retire," or "Already Retired? Learn the Most Effective Income

Preservation Strategies." The visitor will go toward content specifically for them. It's all about benefits, not features.

---

Take a look at your web site's home page. What benefits are highlighted?

_____

_____

_____

_____

---

## A Site that Takes (and Sells!) the Cake

KT Design & Development (www.ktdesign1.com) of Grayslake, Illinois, created the current site for Lovin Oven Cakery, a bakery with two locations in the Chicago area (www.lovinovencakery.com—see Figure 12.1). Lovin Oven's previous site did not have any measurable effects on sales at the bakery. Today, the site generates on average nearly 100 inquiries per month. Owner Ken Slove explained, "Our web site has dramatically improved our customer service abilities—more than almost any tool we've used in our 70-plus year history." The new site was constructed with high priorities of customer service and business development. Here are some of its keys to success:

- *Bolstering their brand identity.* The Lovin Oven Cakery brand is consistently represented throughout the site. The designers created a consistent look for each page using the company colors (red, white, and black), so that customers could readily recognize the business. And since the company wanted frequent visitors to see fresh images, the site has preprogrammed pictures that change automatically for every holiday.
- *Showcasing products.* Lovin Oven hired a professional photographer to shoot the products featured on its web site photo gallery. Since products are its business, the food has to look great—and it does!!

Promoting bakery products and providing excellent customer service at Lovin Oven has become seamless. The new, streamlined process makes the web site the focal point, instead of simply seeing it as a single piece in the puzzle. Customers who have a predetermined idea of how

**Figure 12.1 Lovin Oven**

*Source*: www.lovinovencakery.com

they want to decorate their cake now use the site as a reference tool, and the Lovin Oven sales team uses the site to communicate on the phone with customers who need to see the products being described to them. Wholesale clients use the site to promote the products to their customers, and it enables the bakery to coordinate marketing and advertising efforts seamlessly. But, best of all, Lovin Oven continues to enjoy a consistent increase in sales.

"Our business is booming, despite the economic downturn," said Slove. "We opened a second store in Libertyville in the fourth quarter of 2009, and we've seen the sales at our new store surpass that of our store in Round Lake Beach. The site KT Design & Development built for our business has been a key component of our continued success."

## Your Site Should Be Unique, Just Like Your Firm

An attractive model or stock photography on your site does not tell visitors anything much about who you are. Instead, you want visitors to truly get to know your firm. Powerful tools for doing this include displaying pictures of you and your staff, providing video and audio (using your voice) where you speak to your visitors about your firm, and presenting specific testimonials and/or commentary about the benefits you provide to your target market.

Red Zone Marketing has used Smith & Jones (www.smithnjones .com) in Sturbridge, Massachusetts, for many years for our web site development. The firm has incorporated a variety of unique elements, including an online university (Red Zone University), a modular design, and lots of video. Our web site—www.RedZoneMarketing.com—is the lifeblood of our firm, and continues to drive our benefits (see Figure 12.2). It is now a profit center at the business, not just an online brochure. But it was the addition of video that really became the turning point.

## Video Is a True Differentiator

Video placement on your web site is easier and more effective than ever. You can probably think of a few reasons *not* to use video, but from a marketing perspective, there are so many more compelling reasons that integrating video into your site is an absolute *must*. Some of these benefits include:

- *Video grabs the viewer's attention.* The Internet is filled with text and pictures. Therefore, a short, well-scripted video often stands out to consumers. It helps you build a relationship with people who you may or may not ever meet, and adds a truly personal touch to your web site. This is vital, because the relationship is what keeps customers coming back.

- *Video increases credibility.* Video can make you and your material more believable. Using video on your web site allows you to demonstrate the before and after effects of your product. You can present customer testimonials and encourage your staff to explain products and service information, as well as answer questions. All of this brings increased credibility to you and your company—a significant issue with business today.

- *It's easy.* Almost anyone can create and upload a video. There are dozens of reference sites that make uploading, embedding, and

**Figure 12.2   Red Zone Marketing**
*Source:* www.RedZoneMarketing.com

sharing video almost simple. You don't have to be a professional to do it; in fact, your audience will be a lot happier if you aren't, because it adds a layer of authenticity and credibility.

- *Video is more compelling than text.* Visuals are far better in explaining or presenting information and products than plain text or still pictures and graphics. It is a direct approach that gets to the meaning of what you are saying much more quickly than static text.

- *It has the potential to go viral.* If your video is more than just information and includes a little something extra in terms of entertainment or added humor—it may spread like crazy! (See Chapter 4, "Third Principle: Go Viral!")

What video content could you add to your web site?

_____

_____

_____

_____

## Of Course, *Quality Matters on Your Web Site*

A new business short on investment capital may need to postpone build-ing a top-tier custom web site, so one option is to use a template web site that can be found for minimal cost by searching the Internet. But if your Web presence is critical to your business—and in most cases today, it is— then you should consider investing in a custom site that truly meets your needs. Your web site today is often as important as your office location was years ago. Savvy business owners understand return on investment; they know that investing in a top-tier custom web site can be the cornerstone of a smart business development plan.

Templates cost little (typically less than $100 per month), while many custom sites can total between $10,000 and $25,000, depending on the site specifications. But opting for an inexpensive solution may be a much pricier proposition in the long run—easily costing you $5,000 to $15,000 or more in terms of lost business. And "shortcuts" can actually *hurt* your business. You may invest valuable time—which may have been better spent making new business connections—wrestling with the template. In the end, potential clients will make assumptions about your business based on their initial impression of your site, so it needs to look absolutely pol-ished and professional.

## Expertise Needed in a Web Design Firm

When hiring a professional studio, consider five important areas.[1]

1. Target Marketing

   Work with your developer to determine your site's marketing goals upfront, and clearly identify what you want the site to accom-plish. Pinpoint the specific market targets. Who is your audience? What are the demographics and psychographics of your customer base? What do you really want to sell? Then, every part of your site should be geared back to your target.

What is your site's target audience?

_____

_____

_____

_____

2. Impactful Graphic Design

Your site must make a positive and lasting first impression. The design should reinforce your brand identity, for example, company colors, fonts, and graphics. Include your company logo and make sure the graphics are applied consistently across all media that your company uses—snail mail, e-mail, newsletter, e-zines, presentations, brochures, packaging—*everything*.

What are they key elements in the design of your web site?

_____

_____

_____

_____

3. Professionally Crafted Content

Make sure your message is concise and easy to read. The primary goal of writing is to get the message read and understood. Communicate clearly your product or service's benefits and what distinguishes your company from the competition. Include calls to action that convert casual browsers into new business accounts.

What are the benefits of your product or service?

_____

_____

_____

_____

What distinguishes your company from the competition?

_____

_____

_____

_____

*(continued)*

(*continued*)

Calls to Action

_____

_____

_____

_____

4. Experienced Web Development

Experience is *very* important in getting your site done right, so hire a studio with extensive experience, particularly one that specializes in web development. Ask to see the company's portfolio of client sites, and check references, too. I unfortunately know of more than one business that has paid a deposit for web development to a company that promptly went out of business—resulting in no web site and no refund, and a virtual nightmare!

Reference Check

_____

_____

_____

_____

5. Content Ownership

After the project is completed, ask the studio to release the files to you; otherwise, you will pay every time you make a change to your site. You should always have "administrative access"; this allows you to update the site as needed without incurring additional costs.

What do you want to be able to regularly change on your web site without incurring cost?

_____

_____

_____

_____

## A Good Idea Needs a Great Web Strategy

Brian Hanson started a company he knew nothing about and turned it into a million-dollar venture—all through the use of the Web. Brian and his wife, who are in their twenties, had no capital backing and no college education, yet they wanted to start a recession-proof business. They researched many different types of companies and came upon the auto industry. Not selling cars, but providing parts for cars being serviced. Because people were not buying new cars at the pace they once did, they needed to fix the cars they already had. The Hansons started a company called Got Engines that supplies used, remanufactured, and rebuilt auto engines. Got Engines started in an 800-square-foot office, and because of their web site—www.GotEngines.com—the company began immediately taking sales left and right from competitors with 20,000-plus-square-foot offices that had been around for 10 to 15 years.

"You are as big as you think you are when you run a business online," Brian Hanson said. "I don't consider myself an automotive expert and I don't think I'm in the automotive industry. I'm a marketer, and I'm in the Internet marketing business." Hanson insists that the reason many of his competitors have failed is because they concentrate on infrastructure, while he is focused on producing buyers.

"My engines are just as good as any competitor's, but think about it this way: if my competitor has the best engines on the planet, and mine were just above average but I know a ton about marketing—who's going to sell more, me or them?" Hanson said. "Is it really about who has the best product; or is it about who knows how to find prospects? I believe that the key is knowing how to sell."

Having a strong Internet presence and making it easy for people anywhere to find his engines has allowed Brian to quickly rise to number one in his industry. He's focused on making his site easy to navigate, his office representatives easy to contact for placing orders, and most of all, he's made his business easy to find. Hanson uses all the available searching mechanisms—including search engine optimization and marketing—to share his business with the world of prospective buyers.

## Search Engine Optimization (SEO)

*Search engine optimization* is the process of improving the volume or quality of traffic to a web site from search engines via natural—or unpaid search results. This is unlike *search engine marketing* (SEM), which deals with paid inclusion (see below). Typically, the higher your site appears in the search results list, the more visitors you will receive from the search engine.

SEO may target different kinds of search, including image, local, video and industry-specific vertical search engines. This gives a site significant web presence. As an Internet marketing strategy, SEO considers how search engines work and what people search for. Optimizing a web site primarily involves editing its content, as well as HTML and associated coding to both increase its relevance to specific keywords and remove barriers to the indexing activities of search engines. SEO tactics may be incorporated into web site development and design. The term "search engine friendly" may be used to describe web site designs, menus, content management systems, images, videos, shopping carts, and other components that have been optimized for the purpose of search engine exposure.

## Simple SEO Tips

There are simple steps you can take to improve your site's searchability to move up on the browser ladder.

- *Keywords are key.* A keyword is a word used in a search engine during its search for relevant web pages. Your keywords will enable people to find you through searches, so make sure you have a unique, keyword-focused title tag on every page of your site. Unless you are a major brand, your business name will probably get few searches, so put it in at the end if you must. You can use a keyword tool like https://adwords.google.com/select/KeywordToolExternal to help generate relevant keywords for your site. And remember to focus on search phrases, not single keywords. Put your location in your text to help you get found in local searches.

- *Content is king.* You must have informative, well-written, and unique content that will focus on your primary keyword or keyword phrase.

- *Fresh content can help improve your rankings.* Add new, useful material to your pages on a regular basis. Content freshness adds relevancy to your site in the eyes of the search engines. If your site content doesn't change often, your site needs a blog—because search spiders like fresh text. Update your blog at least three times a week with quality, original content to feed those little crawlers.

- *Link building.* Think quality, not quantity when you build links. A single, authoritative link can do a lot more for you than a dozen poor quality links, which can actually hurt you.

- *Test your SEO effectiveness.* You can test your web site's SEO effectiveness by going to a web site grader site like www.WebSiteGrader .com or www.MySiteGrader.com. These free tools measure a web site's marketing effectiveness by providing a score that incorporates web site traffic, SEO, social popularity, and other technical factors. They also provide some basic advice on how your web site can be improved to increase your SEO.

### Paid Search Engine Marketing

Search engine marketing, or SEM, is a form of Internet marketing that seeks to promote web sites by increasing their visibility in search engine result pages (SERPs) through the use of paid placement, contextual advertising, and paid inclusion. Sites like Google, Yahoo!, Bing—and dozens more—all have SEM programs.

## Evaluate Your Site Using Analytics

Your web site's success is often measured by your "web conversion rate"; in other words, the amount of visitors that you convert into customers. You need to nudge prospects to connect with your site so that they eventually take the action you want. A way to encourage this interaction is to offer potential customers something of value in exchange for filling out information, like a free report or newsletter. You can also give them the option to request a complimentary analysis from your firm, or download some sought-after free information.

Use Google Analytics (www.google.com/analytics) to statistically evaluate your site. Here, you can find out if people searched for your site and what keywords they used. You'll discover how long people stayed on your site, where exactly they went when they arrived, and if they were repeat or new visitors. You can then use the information to continue to improve certain aspects of your web site.

## Get Affiliates to Promote Your Products and Services

Affiliate marketing is a form of online marketing where one web site drives traffic to another. The business receiving the traffic rewards affiliates for each web site visitor or customer brought about by that affiliate's marketing efforts. An affiliate marketing campaign could reach many more potential clients than a simple in-house initiative ever could.

Determine how much you would be willing to invest by "rewarding" your affiliates who refer business to you. Often, the commissions are 50 percent of the product price.

Some businesses have been successful using a multitiered approach. They will have a fundamental package or service at the front end, which they are willing to use as a loss leader. This product or service will lead to more expensive products or services, and require a carefully crafted call to action as well as a natural progression to entice the leading product's purchaser to buy the bigger package. This approach would offer the affiliate a higher commission—maybe even 75 percent—to sell your lead-in product. This certainly motivates the affiliate, and if you have structured your sales funnel correctly, you should be able to use the loss leader as an investment toward larger returns.

There are a number of affiliate marketing networks, some of which specialize in particular niches and others that concentrate in upscale. One is www.LinkShare.com, which provides online marketing solutions in the areas of search, lead generation, and affiliate marketing.

Conduct some of your own online research to determine the best solution for your particular product or service. Make sure that you spend some time creating your sales copy, banner ads, and e-mail content for your affiliates to use. The easier you make it for them to promote your site and services, the more successful your campaign will be.

---

Who are potential affiliates that could drive traffic to your web site?

_____

_____

_____

_____

---

## Other Methods of Bringing Visitors to Your Web Site

Traffic is the lifeblood of your Internet business. Failing to get people to visit your web site makes it unlikely that your business will profit. However, this is a challenge that most marketers experience, and the ones who ⸻⸻ skill will end up running a successful business. Here are a few ⸻ successful strategies.

⸻ *marketing.* Write an article and submit it to major article direc⸻ like www.ezinearticles.com, and include a link to your web site in the resource box. If somebody likes what you have written, they are likely to click through to your web site.

- *Forum marketing*. This method will prompt traffic to your site within minutes of making a post. The key here is to respond to other people who ask for help. Make a valuable contribution and include a link to your web site in your signature.

- *Press releases*. If you have a noteworthy event to mention—the launch of a new product or service, for example—write a press release, and submit it to popular online sites like www.PRWeb.com. If your event is significant enough, it may also be published on the media outlet web sites, or get picked up by search engines for additional traffic.

---

### Take 15 and Get Your Clients Going Wild!
### *A 15-Minute Client-Builder Exercise*

- What changes will you make to your web site right now?

  _____

  _____

  _____

- What changes will you make to your web site over the next year?

  _____

  _____

  _____

  _____

- How will your prospects find you?

  _____

  _____

  _____

  _____

CHAPTER

13

# Social Media

## Effective Strategies that *Don't* Consume All of Your Time

### The Power of Social Media Is Everywhere

Barack Obama's presidential win was fueled by social media and viral marketing efforts that are credited for getting the youth to vote—a task that has been nearly impossible prior to this election. By the time he was inaugurated in January 2009, the president had 13 million people on his e-mail list, 3 million online donors, 5 million connections on more than 15 different social networking sites (including 3 million Facebook friends), 8.5 million monthly visitors to MyBarackObama.com, nearly 2,000 official YouTube videos (with more than 80 million views and 135,000 subscribers), and more than 3 million people signed up for his text messaging program. Astonishing—and obviously quite effective.

Business owners need to unlock the power of social media as a means of spreading the word about their product and services. But is social media right for *your* business? Is it a viable alternative to traditional marketing and advertising?

The answer depends on your business, your target audience, where your target audience spends their time, and on *you*. Traditional advertising and marketing is not dead, but an integrated approach that combines the traditional with social media is a healthy strategy. The extent to which you add social media to your marketing mix will vary in regard to your particular situation and company. Working through this chapter and its exercises will help you formulate your plan.

## What Really Is Social Media?

Social media is the act of sharing content between online social networks. It began with online discussion forums and opinion sites, and has expanded to include video sharing (YouTube), photo sharing (Flickr) and microblogging (Twitter) sites. Social networking sites such as Facebook and LinkedIn are driving the collaborative nature of the medium. To that end, Social Media Marketing (SMM) is the practice of creating compelling online content from a marketing angle that can help to increase visitors to a web site, and ultimately enhance business under the right conditions.

### Social Media Is Immediate
Traditional media is regulated by time and space constraints. There is almost always more information than is possible to be released, which forces professionals who work in those mediums to tailor their messages to the space available. Traditional media also has deadlines that dictate when messages can be delivered. The "always on" world of social media is dramatically different, however; there are no restrictions, rules, or deadlines in terms of time and space.

### Social Media Is Measurable
Social media users share more than just their opinion—they share many clues about who they are and how they think via information found in social bookmarks, comments, engagement, influence, friends, followers, downloads, favorites, views, votes, and links. These user actions allow you to measure what's important, what ideas are gaining ground and who—or what—is having the biggest impact on your or your client's brand.

### Active Participation Is the Key
Many companies have embraced Facebook, LinkedIn, Twitter, and YouTube by diligently creating their profile pages—and then waiting for the business to flood in. However, despite the hype, social media is not a get-rich-quick scheme. If you don't have a group of people paying attention to what you are posting and are ready to share it with others, it will just sit there.

If you want to attract new visitors via social media, drive traffic to your web site, and ultimately sell something, you have to actively participate. Becoming involved in online conversations, delivering and sharing valuable content, and regularly interacting in a community are the first steps to getting involved. But, before you begin to devote all of your free time to social media, ask yourself if it can really help your business.

### Social Media Can Be Internal

Teach for America is a non-profit organization whose mission is to eliminate educational inequity by enlisting recent college graduates from all backgrounds and career interests to commit to teach for two years in underserved urban and rural public schools. Teach for America provides the training and ongoing support necessary to ensure their success as teachers in low-income communities. Their teachers, also called corps members, have a mission to go above and beyond traditional expectations to lead students to significant academic achievement, despite the challenges of poverty and the limited capacity of the school system.

In an effort to facilitate teacher communication and collaboration across the United States, Teach For America has developed a network of support and resources that help corps members quickly move up the learning curve. As a result, corps members have the tools needed to become excellent teachers and make a greater impact on students than typically would be expected in a year. To enable and encourage collaboration with their 25,000 teachers and alumni, they have developed their own social extranet called TFAnet.org, powered by Lotus Connections, a business software solution for collaborative work environments.

"We used to communicate through thousands of spreadsheets that were constantly being updated to keep them current. Now we have a true resource exchange for our teachers," said Ellen Shepard, SVP, Chief Information Officer of Teach for America. "Teachers have a network they can access anytime where they can view teacher profiles, communicate and exchange ideas, and have access to curriculums and subjects. Their ability to connect and communicate with one another also serves to fuel the mission while increasing teacher effectiveness."

## Social Media Business Benefits

If you want to get more involved in social media, it's helpful to consider some of the positive returns that you could derive from a well-structured campaign. Some of the benefits of social media are:

- *Low cost method to get the word out about your company and products.* Your social media strategy is an extremely low-budget, sometimes free, replacement or compliment to traditional advertising and marketing. You likely can reach the same target audience for a fraction of the cost.

- *Exposure for your brand.* A successful social media marketing campaign leads to augmented discussion of your brand online. When your message resonates with your users, they will spread it more effectively than traditional methods might.

- *Immediate gratification.* Exposure on the front page of major social videos, news, or bookmark sites has the potential to send huge amounts of traffic almost instantly to your web site. And although traffic doesn't always equate to sales, it does generate momentum in the right direction.

  For example, social news web sites like Digg have been known to send upward of 40,000 unique visitors to web sites shortly after they appear on the Digg.com front page. If your story doesn't get to the front page, then you are unlikely to see much more than a handful of visitors. Everything on Digg—from news to videos to images—is submitted by visitors. Once something is posted, by you or someone else, other people see it and vote or "Digg" what they like best. If your submission receives enough Diggs, it is promoted to the front page for the millions of daily visitors to see.

- *Impact on search engine ranking.* Social media can generate large amounts of backlinks—incoming links to a web site or web page— that benefit your search engine ranking. The number of backlinks is one indication of the popularity or importance of that web site or page.

- *Create influencers.* Social media can create an army of people that may recommend your company. These influencers can have dramatic effects on sales from a simple recommendation—one that is broadcast to the world. It has been equated to the power Oprah has on TV.

- *Increase sales.* You can ultimately increase your sales by creating more exposure for your product and service. If done correctly, social media gives you methods to gain extraordinary coverage.

## So What's the Catch?

After considering some of social media's advantages, you may be asking yourself what else you should be doing, and how you can benefit from social media. But the only way—and I mean the *only* way—that social media works is if you have compelling content (see Chapter 4, "Third

Principle: Go Viral!"). People will not share your information, writing, videos, or pictures unless they are interesting. So your first step in getting involved in social media in a more impactful way is to constantly come up with material that you feel others will find appealing, valuable, helpful, shocking, or inspiring.

## What Is "Interesting"?

Fencing supply company Louis E. Page significantly increased its sales leads after starting a blog. When owner Duncan Page posted a blog entry about how to use woven wire fencing to build a horse paddock, he was surprised to find that that entry alone attracted more than 1,500 views. The result: traffic, media coverage, and an 850 percent increase in sales leads. You have to figure out what may be interesting or unique to your potential customers.

---

What's some interesting content you could begin sharing online?

_____

_____

_____

_____

---

## Social Media Tools

There are thousands of social media tools. These are some of the more popular sites for business.

*Blog.* If you want to build a following, start blogging. Creating a blog site is free. You can connect it to your web site and e-mail newsletters, and it becomes your online voice. Some sites that can help you create a blog are TypePad, Blogger, and HubSpot. (Red Zone Marketing uses TypePad.) Blogging disseminates information about a company in a way that goes beyond a formal press release, ad, marketing brochure, or web site. This is the place to display material *and* invite people's perspectives, as it provides an opening for real relationships to be formed and can be integral in fostering brand loyalty.

Each blog entry should be short and take no longer than an hour to write. Blogs that are refreshed regularly get a boost in search engine rankings and can help to establish you as an authority—for free.

*LinkedIn.* LinkedIn is a social networking site for business-to-business networking. It's where the Fortune 500 appears online; in fact, executives representing every member of the Fortune 500 are on this site. The average household income of LinkedIn users tops $100,000 per year. This web site is a lot like a living resume, because many people visit it to search for a name before doing business with that person. Individuals should keep their LinkedIn profile up-to-date and not be afraid to ask others for recommendations after they have done business with a particular person or group. For many, proper management of LinkedIn profiles acts as a nonstop sales promotion of you and your brand.

LinkedIn also lets users connect with others who are also looking to create partnerships or collaborate. The site allows you to establish and/or join special interest groups and comment in discussions within the groups. Digests from these groups and conversations are delivered by e-mail to group members on a daily or weekly basis.

*Facebook.* Though Facebook initially began as a social networking tool primarily for students, the site eventually gained traction with non-academic users—and is now the most active social network on the Web. Think of Facebook as a social media headquarters, and use it as a virtual clearinghouse. Facebook allows you to easily push your content—blog, press releases—from various social sites, and is a great place to host a conversation. You can engage your audience almost immediately by using your personal profile, fan pages, and the groups you have at your disposal. Facebook users designate their likes and dislikes, add applications, join groups, and attend events of interest to them. All of this information is right there on their page for you to see.

*Twitter.* Twitter is a microblogging site that is growing at an extremely rapid pace. Many people use Twitter to post thought-provoking links or ask questions. Content on Twitter is about quality—not quantity. You only have 140 characters to get your point across, so the material that you promote—not the number of words that you use—is what will do all of your talking. Twitter can also be utilized as a platform to have direct conversations with followers. A recent news story told about a doctor leveraging Twitter to communicate to his patients and peers about his practice's news and updates.

Once you establish a Twitter account, you may find yourself asking how to find the people you need to follow. Twitter search is the best way to seek out other users who are engaged in the conversations of interest to you and your brand. Because Twitter search is not fully integrated into the Twitter Web experience, you can use http://search.twitter.com. Simply type in keywords related to your business or industry, and you'll quickly get a real-time glimpse into active conversations.

*YouTube.* Another way to capitalize on the fast pace of social media is by posting videos on YouTube. With a little creativity and relatively low overhead (Flip video cameras can be had for as little as $100), uploading a short clip can be a rapid and effective way to test the market. Video also adds a personal touch that allows your customers to see and hear you, as opposed to simply reading your name and information about your brand. It's is a great way to build trust with your users. A weekly Vlog (video blog post) uploaded from your site to YouTube can really tap into this market, and, again, build trust with your users.

An added bonus for YouTube submission is that videos play a major role in Google's Universal Search algorithm, which gives preference to video content that is popular on YouTube and other video-sharing services. Google, in turn, presents these videos along with search results. This can increase your search engine rankings and bring forth an additional stream of traffic. YouTube videos are easily monetized if you prefer to do so by selling sponsorships and adding a short "shout-out" in the beginning or end of the video.

## Strategies for Gaining Followers

If you create great content, but no one is listening—you haven't left the starting blocks with social media. There are several tactics to get people following you and what you say; but remember, without valuable information, they won't stick around for long. Here are seven tips.

1. *Create accounts where your clients and prospects are already visiting.* Though most businesspeople today use LinkedIn, Facebook, and Twitter, there are many more options. You need to find out where your customers and potential customers are gathering, and choose your social media outlet based on what fits your target market best.

2. *Create an effective avatar.* Your avatar is your personal online brand. Create one that doesn't look like you shot it with a camera phone in your bathroom mirror. Use a simple, informal, straight-up picture. When people view your social media conversations, your avatar should stand out.

3. *Search for friends and contacts with whom to connect.* If you are looking for others in the business with which you are associated—for example, financial services—then search for terms like "financial advisor" or "financial service firms." Invite potential contacts to connect with you.

4. *Keep them coming back.* Now that you have established a database of friends or followers, you need to make sure they return for more of your valuable material. Create unique content, share value, and post weekly blogs to keep followers coming back for more.

   "Establish yourself as a subject expert," says cofounder of Alltop .com, former chief evangelist for Apple Inc., and author of nine books including *Reality Check* (Portfolio, 2008) Guy Kawasaki. "That way, you'll be interesting to some subset of people. Say you're an expert on Macintosh. Search for 'Macintosh' and answer people's questions. People are likely to not only follow you, but also retweet your posts, giving you additional exposure." Kawasaki also notes, "If and when you're an expert, don't be afraid to express your opinion. It's better that some people refuse to follow you than no one knows who you are."

5. *Blog, blog, blog.* Blogging is the best way to convey your content. You can use the other social media tools to drive people to your blog, and ultimately your web site. Video blogging is another way of generating interest; but always make sure that all of your social media sites automatically update when you make a new blog post or video submission. This is easily done with all of the tools that are now coming out on an almost daily basis.

6. *Update your web site to include and integrate your social media sites.* You want your customers to see a social media presence on your homepage that directs them and other interested people to several outlets to where they can interact with you: LinkedIn, Twitter, Facebook, and so forth. You'll also want to include links to promotional videos posted on hosting sites like YouTube, which should be one of the top tools for PR.

7. *Go from online to face-to-face.* Transitioning from online conversations to sales is the ideal result in social media, and because sales conversions are usually conducted face-to-face, you might consider hosting an event for your followers. Twitter users call this a "tweetup"—which, according to a definition by PCMag.com, is a gathering of users brought together via Twitter. For example, Twitter is used by conference attendees to arrange to meet after the show for discussion, cocktails, and parties.

## Using Social Media Tools to Increase Loyalty and *Save* Money

There is rapidly increasing demand for qualified individuals to design, implement, and maintain advanced networking technology. For example, network equipment and management supplier Cisco's Networking

Academy is a global education program that teaches students how to design, build, troubleshoot, and secure computer networks for increased access to career and economic opportunities throughout global communities. The program provides hard technical and soft-skills training to ensure that students are well-prepared for job roles, and so there is a solid pipeline of talent available for customers and partners.

Cisco's Online Community Strategist Charlie Treadwell (Charlie @ Cisco) created a Facebook fan page to connect students beyond their courses to expand reach, increase awareness of the global program, and assist knowledge sharing and interaction within the worldwide student community. The use of social media has enabled Cisco to expand the program's scope and visibility while facilitating information sharing and community interaction.

Within six months of the fan page's launch, Cisco had more than 37,000 engaged Facebook fans. One of the most valuable discoveries, however, has been the number of content experts that dedicate their time to supporting the community. And Charlie @ Cisco's sudden fame has been a remarkable surprise as well. At a conference in July 2009, Treadwell was socializing with a group of academy instructors when one of them stopped him in mid-sentence, looked at his nametag, and said, "Are you Charlie at Cisco?" And the page had only been live for one month.

One of the largest costs in running an online education program is managing the questions and feedback necessary to give students a complete education. Cisco's bottom line has benefited in several ways.

"While trying to quantify the value of our customer community, I looked at the cost to maintain our help desk," said Treadwell. "It costs us approximately $23 every time one of our students or instructors contacts our support desk via e-mail, phone, or live chat. That can be resolved [in each instance] through community support on Facebook—and save us $23. Even if someone would have not contacted our support desk but rather found the help they needed online, we could quantify the value in the service that had been offered to them."

The site has facilitated a community-learning environment. An example is when one of the more dedicated members created tutorial videos to answer frequently asked questions—and has even started taking requests for topics of future videos. With some students isolated in small classrooms across the globe, this "right now" help has undoubtedly led to higher retention rates, and offers students the study support that they need.

"We are investigating how to best identify community members that could make great public ambassadors, to cultivate a large community of intrinsically motivated experts," Treadwell said. "We are also looking to improve the functionality of our social media activities to allow for users to search the conversations and reduce the amount of questions that have already been answered."

## Monitor Your Brand Online

Monitoring is the first step to determining whether your social media efforts are garnering results. In an article appearing on Mashable .com, Social Media Specialist Dan Schawbel at EMC Corporation said, "Brand monitoring has become an essential task for any individual or corporation."

When people talk about you or your company these days, it's out there for everyone to see. Word-of-mouth advertising was just a whisper 10 years ago compared to what it is today because of online message travel. Conversations about you and your company—either positive or nega-tive—may happen on the web whether you like it not. And the key is not to fight it or ignore it, but to address your web reputation head on; because these conversations can *dramatically* impact your brand.

For instance, Comcast has a Twitter account entitled @comcastcares to help Comcast users in need. It's constantly monitored as a way to hear about and respond to customer issues. If you complain about Comcast on-line, you can be sure that @comcastcares will lend a helping hand.

Similarly, Red Zone Marketing has hired a staff member whose sole responsibility is online strategy. Her title is "Director of Online Reputa-tion," and she coordinates everything from our multiple blogs, article placements on other blogs, community sites, book reviews, multiple social media accounts, e-mail newsletter to affiliate marketing. I write all the content, personally respond to all connections, and approve all content going live, and the director manages the process. Not only is it a full-time job for our company, it is a profit center.

## Create Your Brand Reputation System Using Monitoring Tools

Chris Brogan is president of New Marketing Labs, a new media marketing agency. He works with large and mid-sized companies to improve online business communications through the use of social software, community platforms, and other emerging web and mobile technologies. Brogan has written about prioritizing social media efforts in order to most effectively use available resources. He suggests measuring your progress through the

use of monitoring software and a dashboard. *Everything*, Brogan emphasizes, should be tracked.

Software programs like Scoutlabs and Radian6—both web-based
applications—find and monitor signals occurring in the world of
social media. They allow you to follow what people are saying in your
industry, keep an eye out for trends, and listen to customer feedback. It
truly is easier than ever today to stay ahead of the game—you can learn
of people's opinions across large sections of the population. And when
you listen to what is being said, you will find signals for what to pay
attention to, what customers are ranting and raving about, and what's
new and emerging.

Online expert Dan Schawbel—author of *Me 2.0: Build a Powerful
Brand to Achieve Career Success* (Kaplan, 2009)—suggests using social media monitoring tools to protect your reputation. Here is a list of some tools
that are available for free:

- Google Reader

    Schawbel recommends that you establish a central hub for all on-
    line brand coverage with a feed reader like Google Reader (www
    .Google.com/reader). RSS—most commonly known as "Really Sim-
    ple Syndication"—is a web feed format used to publish blog entries,
    news headlines, audio, and video in a standardized format. Feed read-
    ers gather the RSS feeds by constantly checking your selected favor-
    ite news sites and blogs for fresh content. Whenever a site updates, it
    will appear in one place, acting as a personalized inbox for the entire
    Web. You can access a Google Reader account from any computer or
    most mobile phones with online access.

- Delicious

    Delicious (www.Delicious.com) is a social bookmarking service
    where you can save all of your bookmarks online, share them with
    other people, and see what others are bookmarking. It also displays
    the most popular bookmarks being saved right now across various
    areas of interest, and can help sort and organize blogs that mention
    your brand. Delicious is like a personal research and development
    center for your brand.

- Google Alerts

    Google Alerts (www.Google.com/alerts) are e-mail updates of the
    latest relevant Google results based on your choice of query. You can
    subscribe to each alert through e-mail and RSS. The alerts track blog
    posts, news articles, videos, and even groups. Set a "comprehensive
    alert" for your name, your topic, and even your company to receive
    notifications of stories as they happen.

- Technorati

  If you have a blog, Schawbel says, you *must* be on Technorati (www.Technorati.com), an Internet search engine for searching blogs. When you register your blog with Technorati, it tracks blog reactions or blogs that link to yours. Search for your brand on Technorati, and subscribe to RSS alerts so that you can find out when someone blogs about you.

- Backtype

  Backtype (www.Backtype.com) is a tool for monitoring blog comments. Whenever someone cites your name online, Backtype will find it, so use it to know about and join in on conversations. And whenever you write a comment with a link to your web site, Backtype attributes it to you.

- Boardtracker

  Discussion boards are another source for people to comment about you. Boardtracker (www.Boardtracker.com) gives you instant alerts from any comment string that cites your name.

- Social Oomph

  Twitter messages or tweets that people send about you move *fast*. In order to catch them, you can use a service like Social Oomph (www.SocialOomph.com) to set up and track keywords in the public Twitter stream. The free service monitors the Twitter tweet stream and periodically e-mails you a digest of the tweets that contain those keywords. You can also use this to track your @replies. Additionally, Social Oomph will allow you to send an automatic direct message to someone who has followed you, and provides other time-saving tools as well.

- Test the quality of your offering

  The power of the Internet can be positive or negative, so make sure that you are offering something of quality, or your efforts may potentially backfire. Experts recommend testing your product out before running an entire campaign around it—and be prepared to listen and respond to your customers. This is a two-way conversation, much like an informal focus group, that will allow you to understand your customers' views and concerns relating to your products.

## Social Media Time Management

With any small business, time management is an important—if not critical—factor in success. Depending on your product or service, you may find it more efficient to allocate a larger portion of your already stretched time on a few targeted social media sites, rather than spreading yourself too thinly across multiple sites.

List your priority mediums for updates and follow up (Facebook, LinkedIn, Twitter, and so on)

1. _____
   _____
2. _____
   _____
3. _____
   _____
4. _____
   _____
5. _____
   _____

Next, set up your tracking tools (see free monitoring tools above).

Select your brand management tracking tools and methods (Google Alerts, Technorati, Social Oomph, and so on)

1. _____
   _____
2. _____
   _____
3. _____
   _____

Then set up a schedule for interacting.

### Determine the Time You Will Spend Using Social Media

By setting specific days and times to focus on social media, you will be able to effectively add this kind of marketing without letting it take over your day—or worse, pushing it aside for days.

- *Weekly?* (Set Time) – Or –
- *Daily?* (Set Time) – Or –
- *Multiple Times Daily* (Set Times)

**Take 15 and Get Your Clients Going Wild!**
*15-Minute Client-Builder Exercise*

Once a month, review the following (and add in a few more of your own).

1. Review and discuss effectiveness of your social media activities.
2. Assess progress toward your goals.
3. What are your next steps?

CHAPTER

## 14

# Permission-Based Marketing

## Strategies for Successful E-Mail and E-Newsletters

*To be successful you must create a quality message that recipients just can't bring themselves to delete.*

L ike all those other things that have fallen out of favor over the years—acid-washed jeans, VCRs, fax machines—the good old days of welcomed e-mail messages are over. Yes, not too long ago, many of you would have been excited about getting a new e-mail—now you look at your inbox and want to cry. How many times have you found yourself exclaiming at your desk—either to yourself or anyone who will listen—"*Forty new messages in the past hour! How is that possible?!?*"

The reality is that e-mail has become one of your main methods of communication, and as a result, you get a lot of it. Unfortunately, to get to the truly relevant messages, you frequently have to sift through a lot of junk. On any given day, you might find out you inherited money from the King of Nairobi or be asked to forward a message to 10 of your friends, or risk permanent bad luck.

These kinds of junk marketing e-mails are the enemy for professionals who use or want to use permission-based marketing to promote their

174

business. This "spam" is the reason customers and potential customers automatically hit delete when they see a message from an unknown e-mail address, and they are the standard you absolutely *must* avoid when developing your permission-based marketing campaigns.

## Permission-Based Marketing

"Permission-based marketing" is a term that was coined to explain a marketing technique that requires the recipient to give permission before receiving any marketing materials or advertisements. In some cases, the recipient has given permission directly to a company; while in others he or she may have simply searched for a product online—which counts as giving permission in the twenty-first century!

The most common form of permission-based marketing used in today's market is e-marketing. And when used correctly, e-mail and e-newsletters can be valuable marketing tools.

To be successful in this arena, you must create a quality message that recipients simply can't bring themselves to delete. Blanketing a list with a haphazardly created message will not work. However, presenting well-written copy, an intuitive design, and material that people care about will allow you to create permission-based marketing that might end up being one of the best business investments you ever make.

## Two "Es" in a Pod: E-Mail and E-Newsletters

There are two main ways to directly market your company using permission-based marketing: e-mail and e-newsletters. The one you use—or whether you should consider a combination of the two—to increase your business success depends on a variety of factors, including your company's particular marketing needs and the results you want to achieve. But before you get send-happy, there are a few key points to keep in mind to ensure that your e-marketing campaign is poised to achieve optimal results.

### Building a Great List

The list you use for your e-marketing campaign can be built in a variety of ways. For example, you can sponsor a giveaway or offer free information or products in exchange for a person's contact information. You can also advertise your e-newsletter on your web site to entice users to sign up. Or you can just ask! When you've closed business with a new client, when you are checking someone out at the register, or when someone is using your online store—these are all opportunities to provide customers and clients with an opportunity to opt-in to your e-marketing list. Trade shows and organizational meetings are other great places to make new contacts and find people who may be interested in what you have to offer. From now on, whenever you meet new contacts, ask politely for their e-mail address and for permission to send them your e-mail updates or e-newsletter.

If you are starting from the ground up with no contacts of your own, then you might want to consider purchasing a list of people who may have an interest in your particular product or service. However, this can be a risky move, because these people have not yet agreed to receive e-mails from you. In this case, you need to take special care to ensure that your e-mails entice them to respond to you and opt in to additional information.

Organize your list by what each person may be interested in receiving. If you bombard the people on your list with news or updates that aren't attuned to their specific interests or preferences, you run the risk of getting unsubscribe requests from people who might have been interested in your future e-blasts. And whatever you do, make sure that any e-marketing strategies you use are well within the legal and courteous guidelines. Nothing will turn a potential client off more than being *spammed* against their will. Take a hint from those old-school, door-to-door sales callers, and let your customers invite you in before you inundate them with information about your company.

## A Closer Look at E-Mail

E-mail is a marketer's dream: It's inexpensive, user-friendly, and efficient. It allows you to send and receive information within seconds. You can use it to make an announcement, send out recent press materials and media hits about your company, or simply connect with clients and others interested in your particular industry. You can even use certain programs to see who opens your e-mails (and who isn't!), who clicks through the links you provide, and exactly how effective your campaign actually is.

E-mail allows you to reach the masses with a simple click. It saves you time, resources, and money. It's also one of the most preferred methods of contact for consumers, since it allows them to view materials at their own convenience, thereby avoiding interruptions to their own workday.

### Getting Your Mail Opened

With the abundance of e-mail that people receive these days, it's important to make sure that yours stands out from the crowd by doing the following:

- *Deliver on your promises.* The best way to ensure that your messages are always opened is to put your money where your mouth is. If you promise one thing in your subject line, you'd better make sure the content of your e-marketing message backs it up. For example, let's say you run a shoe store. If your last e-blast promised "A Great New Offer!" in the subject line, and your recipients opened the message to find an offer that read, "For a limited time only, buy any one pair of shoes and receive the second pair free!"—well, your customers would probably agree that that is *indeed* a great offer. You can rest assured that those recipients will be sure to open up the next e-mail they see from your store.

- *Make the subject line sing.* As mentioned before, most people's inboxes are already overflowing. Getting them to open your message requires a clever subject line—one that catches the recipient's attention. Try to create subject lines that are eye-catching and provocative, and that make statements that make readers feel as though they *have* to open your e-mails to see what's inside. Even better, tie your subject lines to current events or hot topics. This is a great way to pique people's interest and garner results. Here are some I've seen:
  - Top 10 Vacation Spots in the United States
  - Most viewed videos on YouTube
  - Business Building Workshop Super Special Discount

- *Consistency, consistency, consistency.* One of the best ways to create a loyal following is to make it easy for your subscribers to recognize you. Be sure that you always send your e-marketed messages out at the same time each day, week, or month so that your readers will know when to expect your e-newsletters and updates. Doing so will make it easier for them to pick your messages out of the crowd. Additionally, try using similar language or formatting in your subject lines. If readers know to look for your update on Tuesdays, then they will be less likely to hit "delete" when they see an overcrowded inbox in the morning.

## Delivering Value

Now that you know how to get your e-mail marketing communications opened, let's see how you can ensure that you are consistently delivering great messages that the people on your list won't be able to resist.

- *Content matters most.* Bottom line: If you convey quality content in a way that is pleasing to the eye, your recipients will always give your messages a chance. Messages with crisp, snappy copy are entertaining for recipients and a pleasure to read. Make sure your messages are specifically tailored to those on your list. Always provide them with something that matters to them—whether it's a coupon, relevant information on an emerging industry trend, or product updates.

And please—don't sweat it if you're not a great writer. Hire a copywriter to help you tailor your messages. The added cost will be well worth it when you start receiving new business inquiries based on your messages.

- *Keep it short and sweet.* One of the reasons that e-mail is the preferred method of communication is because it fits well in the busy lives we so commonly keep. If people opt in to be contacted by e-mail only, it usually means that their schedules are jam-packed. They are too busy to take time out of the day for a phone call, and they are also probably too busy to spend all day reading e-mails. Just because you could fill a book with information on how great your company is, it doesn't mean you should—and certainly not via e-mail. Keep your message short and to the point. Put the most important headlines in boldface font so that readers will catch what you're trying to say, even if they are just skimming your e-mail. They will appreciate the time you've saved them, and will reward you by opening your e-mails on a regular basis.

### Use a Professional Service

From Constant Contact to Bronto to Magnet Mail, there is no shortage of companies out there that can help you make the most of your e-mails. Not only can these services assist you in formatting your e-mails and managing your ever-growing list, they can also keep you up-to-date on your campaign's analytics. They offer the additional advantages of a suppression list—a function that keeps a database of all e-mail addresses of people who have opted out—and prevents them from receiving any future e-mails from you.

### Make Your Message Mobile Friendly

With the growing popularity and advancement of PDAs and other mobile devices, users can access their e-mails anywhere, at any time. The good news is that your message will reach your customers much faster. They don't have to wait until they are back in their offices to see what you have to say. The bad news is that not all graphics, designs, or formatted e-mails will show up on these devices, and they can even make them hard to open. E-mail marketing messages work because they are quick and easy to access. But if yours are causing recipients problems on their PDAs, it may prompt them to unsubscribe.

### Consider Using E-Mail in Your Never-Ending Quest for Referrals

E-mail your top clients to ask them if they have friends or colleagues who may be interested in your services; or, include a link on your web site inviting clients to join your "referral" club. Explain that they would receive special privileges or some sort of gift in exchange for some promising leads. Just the fact that you asked means you view them as "important" and trust their judgment. What better way to build a strong, mutually beneficial relationship?

### Send a Survey

You might be thinking, *no one will take the time to fill out a survey!* But don't be so quick to dismiss them; they are actually a great way to get your recipients' attention. First of all, remember that you will be blasting this survey to the hundreds—maybe even thousands—of people on your list. Even if only a third or a fourth of them respond, you've succeeded; because those who did will have provided useful feedback about your company, or told you what they would like to receive from your company. *And* you've just made them feel a little more connected to your company. There are many free online survey companies, including www.SurveyMonkey.com.

Make sure when creating your survey that it is relatively short, and always tell recipients about how long it will take them to complete—*take this five-minute survey now.* A great way to garner more responses is to offer an incentive for completing it. Create an e-coupon that goes out to all the people who participate, or enter them into an online drawing for a bigger prize.

As always, *content is king.* Don't ask your recipients trivial questions. Make sure that with every question, your survey participants will give you valuable information about how *you* can better serve *them.*

### Respect the Unsubscribe Request

First of all, you should make it as easy as possible for people to unsubscribe. Don't provide a link to unsubscribe that takes them on a labyrinthine quest to actually get their name off the list. A great option for collecting unsubscribers is to simply ask them to respond with a "Please remove me from your list" to the message you've sent them.

Second—and I can't stress this point enough—if someone asks to be taken off your list, then by all means, *take them off the list immediately!* And if someone seems upset or claims that they have made multiple requests to be removed from your list, pick up the phone and have a conversation with them. Apologize for the problem and let them know that you are doing *everything you can* to fix it. A good online reputation is just as important as it is in the "real world"; and you never know when that once-angry consumer will be in the position to recommend your e-newsletter to a colleague who may be interested.

## Taking Big Baby Steps into E-Mail Marketing

Baby Supermall has been a leader in online sales of baby products since 1997. A vast majority of their sales—more than 90 percent—are for baby bedding products. These items are especially hard to resell or up-sell, which leaves Baby Supermall with the challenge of encouraging buyers to purchase again. This led Baby Supermall to establish the following goals for their customer e-mails:

- Increase sales
- Increase the number of repeat visitors
- Create brand awareness

When the company began its campaign, they chose Bronto (www .Bronto.com) to help manage their list and e-mail messages. Baby Supermall's VP of Information Technology Dave Suby initially addressed the company's e-mail list management. He remarked that, "Typically, one-third of our customers opt-in to receive e-mails from us. We also collect about 50 e-mail addresses per week from potential customers who request personal pricing."

"Remailing" has become another tactic that has increased Baby Supermall's sales. "We learned from our Bronto support team that remailing is a great way to increase sales and visibility," said Suby. E-mails are sent to the company's customers every two to three weeks, and then resent to those who fail to open the e-mails one week later. For every remail that Baby Supermall sends, they change the subject line and vary the send time to increase the chance that the recipient will open the e-mail.

Baby Supermall saw immediate results after fully implementing their e-mail marketing program. Although measuring the ability to increase brand awareness is difficult, they can assess these results through e-mail activity. Baby Supermall's average open rate is around 20 percent, and their click-to-open rate is around 40 percent, signaling that they are gaining increased visibility with their customers and ideally, increased mind share.

Baby Supermall also has recorded a 443 percent ROI. Remailing has allowed them to achieve a 150 percent increase in revenue; and on average, its remails generate up to 50 percent of the revenue that was generated from the initial e-mail.

"With the success that we have achieved through e-mail marketing, it's a no-brainer that this is a great solution to help increase sales and improve visibility," said Suby.

## A Closer Look at E-Newsletters

E-newsletters are a great way to reach out to clients and potential customers, but the reality is that although many people do them, few actually do them well. An excerpt of Red Zone Marketing's weekly *Marketing Audibles* e-newsletter is in Figure 14.1. So before jumping into e-newsletters, let's look at some tips from those that are finding success with this marketing strategy.

- *Plan your newsletters in advance.* Plan out the content for your newsletters six months in advance. Research emerging trends or upcoming events, and consider the kind of information that will consistently grab your recipients' attention. Then write the first two months worth of your e-newsletters so that you can start fine-tuning, and so that content is never put together in a hurry. (Remember to always review any content you've written ahead of time to make sure it is still accurate!)

  And be flexible. Just because a topic is supposed to be included in a given newsletter doesn't mean that it's set in stone. If a hot topic comes up that month or week, use it! You can always write about the original idea at another time.

- *Make sure your e-newsletter makes sense for your clients.* Although these kinds of correspondence are extremely cost-effective and easy to send, a poorly thought-out e-newsletter will only annoy clients. Be sure you put the same level of thought into yours as you would a traditional, hard copy newsletter. The bottom line is value. Your monthly, bimonthly, or quarterly e-newsletters must be filled with valuable information for your readers every time—or they will simply stop reading.

- *Don't be afraid to sound like a broken record.* When it comes to getting your message across, consistency is vital. If you've found a particular topic or theme that seems to resonate with the people on your list, don't be afraid to repeat it in your newsletter. If you find a formula that works, by all means, use it again!

**Are Introverts the Better Connectors?**

You might not be the type of person who loves to socialize, attend big parties, and network whenever the opportunity presents itself. But to be a great connector, you don't have to. Successful connectors who would be classified as introverts will often enter into a social situation with a plan for those they want to meet and connect with. They aren't looking to talk to anyone and everyone, but would rather reach out with more purpose, to select individuals. And going into a social situation with a plan almost always produces better results than going into a networking event or other meeting just "winging it". To effectively connect with another person, it doesn't matter whether you are introverted or extroverted; what matters is that you've spent some time thinking about which relationships are most vital, what you are hoping to achieve by reaching out, and having a plan for reaching them effectively.

**Do you have a plan?** Click here to download the free planning tool, *"For Introverts…and Extroverts: A Plan for Connecting"* and become a better connector today!

READ MORE

## Marketing Clinic

**Q & A with Maribeth Kuzmeski**

Q *I really want to write a book, but I find that I don't have the time or focus to sit down and get it going. But I have a great idea and really want to get the book written. How have you written your books? Do you have suggestions for 'getting out of the gate?'* Jack R, Minnesota

A If you are a verbal person and would prefer to talk than write, one way to get your book written is to talk out the ideas. Sometimes the greatest inhibitor is the blank computer screen staring back at us, waiting for brilliance to come. Block out one or two hours each week devoted to your book. First, develop the chapter outline of the book. Then, begin dictating what you know about each chapter – one at a time. You can use www.CopyTalk.com, or a voice recognition software like Dragon Naturally Speaking, or a dictation service. These services allow you to record your ideas not only when you are in front of your computer, but really anywhere. Writing can often be a stop-and-go process where we are not able to record all of our ideas fast enough. Talking them out can lead to a more continuous flow of getting out everything we want to say. Once the dictation comes back, you can edit what you said to perfect it. It is a great way for verbal people to get things written without too much pain!

**Ask your questions and share your successes by emailing** info@redzonemarketing.com

**RZM Special Feature**
What's Your Credibility Worth?
The 2010 Advisor's Credibility Summit
**How to convert your trust and credibility into greater professional success!**

**April 16 & 17, 2010**

**VOLUME 1 • ISSUE 28**
**Recommended Reading**

Drive: The Surprising Truth About What Motivates Us

In *Drive*, Pink examines the three elements of true motivation, and offers smart and surprising techniques for putting these into action. He takes us to companies that are enlisting new approaches to motivation and are pointing a bold way forward.

**The Red Zone Marketing**

## Radio Show

**Listen Now! What's Working in Credit Union Financial Services** - Ben Pahl, multi-million dollar producer, shares his secrets for getting others to network *for* you, a tactic for eliminating appointment cancellations, and more. All in 30 minutes!

**Recent Radio Show Episodes** - Listen Online Anytime!

*Robert Morris, Amazon.com Top 50 Reviewer Interviews Maribeth Kuzmeski!*

**Writing Emails that Get Opened**

Everyone knows how to send an email. But how can you be sure the recipient will even bother to read it?

**The Connectors in the Media!**

Check out the video above to get some quick tips on how to be a better connector in 2010!

**Figure 14.1   Red Zone Marketing's *Marketing Audibles* E-Newsletter**

- *Keep the design consistent.* The design, format, and length of your newsletter should be consistent to help brand yourself. Readers appreciate knowing what to expect from your newsletter. Always be sure to include your contact and unsubscribe information, as well as ways that readers can forward your message to a friend or colleague.

- *Be sure your web site offers the option to opt-in.* Your web site is a great way to boost your e-marketing contact list. Current customers and those who have (happily!) stumbled on your "online office" may be interested in receiving more information via your e-newsletter. All they need to know is how to sign up! Make sure that you clearly display the "Sign up for more information here!" button on your web site; and make signing up an easy process for those who are interested. You may be surprised just how fast your list grows.

- *Keep it the same as with e-mail: short, sweet, and easy to read.* People don't have time to read lengthy articles or sift through tons of information to figure out which parts apply to them. Keep this in mind when you put together your e-newsletter. Don't overcomplicate your subject matter; keep your articles or columns as short as possible. The idea behind the e-newsletter is to pique interest in your product or service in the hopes that consumers will contact you for more information. There will be plenty of time to give the more detailed story later.

- *Make sure your e-newsletter can be easily read on a PDA.* Because of their time-crunched workdays, people will often save e-newsletters to read while they are on the go. If your material won't open or is too difficult to read on a PDA, you will miss out on appealing to these folks. Keep them in mind when you are in the design phase.

## Fill Your E-Newsletter with the "Write" Stuff

There's no doubt that your business is already dedicated to delivering quality products and services to your clientele, so your e-newsletter should be no exception. If clients and other professionals have opted in to receive your e-newsletter, it's important that you take a vested interest in sending them quality materials. If you don't already have a gifted writer on your staff—or if you aren't one yourself—then hire someone to help put it together. If you aren't investing in the materials you are sending out, then you can't expect your clients and potential clients to invest in *you*!

### Give Them Something to Talk About
It's important when brainstorming content for your e-newsletter to think outside the box. Although you certainly want to update your readers on

breaking news and recent industry trends, consider adding content that might make your e-newsletter a little *more* exciting. Try including some interesting or funny stories that are relevant to the topic at hand, or introduce a guest columnist each month. You may even want to have a resources section that suggests books or links to other web sites for further information.

Think about it: If your e-newsletter is a resource people can count on for anecdotes they can share at the next big board meeting or on their sales calls, they'll be sure to open your e-mails time and again.

## Being There When They Need You!

Keeping your company at the top of mind for prospects and clients is one of the reasons that businesses spend the time to create e-mail newsletters. Environmental design company Lorenc+Yoo Design knows that being in the minds of those who can buy when they are ready is critical to their success. Since the need for environmental design services occurs at a company once every few years at most, Lorenc+Yoo wanted to stay in front of their customers and prospects by showcasing the firm's environmental design projects for trade shows, museums, retail spaces, destinations, and resorts.

Lorenc+Yoo Design works with marketing firm Communications 21 (www.c21PR.com) to send out their targeted, quarterly e-newsletter, *Experiential Storytelling* (see Figure 14.2). The results give hope to those hoping to start or improve on their e-mail newsletter. *Experiential Storytelling* regularly exceeds industry standard response rates, and has opened up a channel for regular communication with clients—including regular Request for Proposal requests. The most tangible result, however, was an invitation to bid on a project for UPS for the 2008 Olympics in Beijing, which Lorenc+Yoo won!

Reneé Spurlin, Communications 21's senior account manager, indicates that the planning and focus of the e-newsletter brings consistent successes. "The Lorenc+Yoo list is very targeted [to the] marketing executives and architects responsible for driving traffic and conveying their organizational messages through trade show and museum exhibits and signage," Spurlin said. "We use their language [and] focus on their goals and results instead of [using] 'design speak' and technical information. In addition, Lorenc+Yoo's strives to tell each client's story through [the] design [that's] conveyed in the newsletter—helping to engage readers with compelling images and the story behind every design."

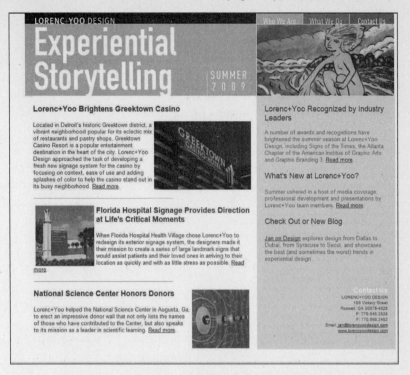

**Figure 14.2    Experiential Storytelling E-Newsletter**
*Source*: www.c21PR.com

## Staying Out of the SPAM Folder

Ending up in the SPAM folder is the kiss of death for any e-marketing piece, so before you send an e-mail or newsletter, be wary of the things that can get your e-mails deleted before they are even opened. All e-mails receive a SPAM rating that is affected by a variety of factors. As your SPAM rating increases, so do the chances of your e-mails being sent directly into the SPAM folder of recipients' e-mails, and thus deleted or ignored. Try using some of these tips and tricks to keep your messages out of the SPAM folder:

- *Watch your words.* Certain keywords—like *win, money, free,* or *promo*—will send e-mails directly to the SPAM folder. Be careful as well about the use of excessive capitalization or punctuation, which are also typically flagged as SPAM.

- *Don't go color crazy.* If you are sending a newsletter or designed e-mail, try to avoid using lots of bold colors or flashy designs. These can result in a higher SPAM score.

- *Know when to invest.* If you are considering using e-mail software, resist saving money by using the cheaper services. These are typically used by spamming companies because of their low cost and e-mails sent using those services will often be automatically flagged.

- *Use a spam-checking service.* The good news is that there is help out there for stopping the SPAM-ban before it starts. Use a spam-checking service like SpamCheck (www.spamcheck.sitesell.com) that can help you to determine if your e-mails are destined for the "forbidden folder." Run all of your e-mails through the service before sending them out, and make any changes ahead of time. It's an easy way to ensure that you stay in the inbox—and your customers' line of sight.

## Pressing Send

Permission-based marketing can be a valuable tool for your business. It's efficient, user-friendly, and—the best part—extremely cost-effective. It's also a great way to communicate with your customers using a method that they quite honestly prefer over other marketing methods

If you take no other lesson from this chapter, let it be this: No matter which strategy you choose, *it's all in the details.* You must pay careful attention to detail to make e-marketing work for you. Know your audiences and respect their level of intelligence; only send messages that you *know* will interest them; and ensure that your copy and designs reflect the quality of work you do.

Follow these important practices and your customers will catch on to your dedication and the high level of work that you do. They will see that your products and services can offer that same level of quality. And that's precisely the message you want to convey.

---

### Take 15 and Get Your Clients Going Wild!
### *A 15-Minute Client-Builder Exercise*

Plan your e-mail newsletter by focusing on target, message, value, and frequency. Write out your objectives and your plan for reaching them.

---

CHAPTER
15

# Traditional Marketing Still Works

## TV and Cable Advertising, Newspaper, and Other Mediums that Still Cause People to Buy

When I make the claim that "traditional marketing still works," it's important that I begin by distinguishing between the tools that are used to *convey* messages—radio, television, newspapers, magazines, billboards, and so forth—and the way these tools are used to deliver messages.

Yes, the traditional tools are still effective, but the ways you can use them have vastly changed. In their book entitled *Punk Marketing*, authors Richard Laermer and Mark Simmons waste no time describing the revolution that has taken place. Published in 2007, the book's prologue begins with the following: "The relationship that consumers have with brands has gone through a seismic shift over the past few years, and a new approach to marketing is long overdue. . . . Smart marketers and all of us businesspeople who rely on marketing realized with a jolt that all was not right in this ever-branded world we paid mightily to live in."

Laermer and Simmons define the term "punk marketing" as "a new form of marketing that rejects the status quo and recognizes the shift in power from corporations to consumers." Technology has indeed given consumers a voice and options they never had before. For instance, an acquaintance of mine who's a devoted hockey fan no longer watches the games on live television. Instead, he records them and watches them later without commercials—in less than half the time it would otherwise take.

Others use TiVo to skip right past commercials, while blogs and other online tools allow consumers to let the world know exactly what they think about certain products or services. A revolution has indeed taken place in the world of marketing, requiring a blend of new messages and the traditional media used to deliver those messages. For more on new media, see Chapter 13, "Social Media."

## Advertising Is *Still* Important

Among the most important methods of delivering your message is advertising. It was the legendary newspaper publisher William Randolph Hearst who offered this advice: "If you make a product good enough even though you live in the depths of the forest, the public will make a path to your door. But if you want the public in sufficient numbers, you would better construct a highway. Advertising is that highway."

And a busy highway it is. Advertising is everywhere you are. There's almost nothing sacred or beyond the reach of advertisers any longer. In the world of sports, advertising messages or logos are painted on athletes' caps, shirts, trousers, and even shoes, as well as on billboards, scoreboards, in stadium signage, promotional sponsorships, cups, bathrooms, and blimps. The game, stadium, and players are all sponsored. Fans watching a single three-hour football game are subjected to hundreds of paid marketing messages—whether they watch the game on TV or live at the stadium.

College football bowl games epitomize this trend. Once upon a time, the college football season ended on January 1 with four bowl games: Rose Bowl, Cotton Bowl, Orange Bowl, and Sugar Bowl. Then, beginning around the early 1970s, more bowl games were gradually added, including the Peach Bowl and the Fiesta Bowl. Today, there are more than 30 bowl games total that are played between mid-December and early January. Most of them—including the original "Big Four"—now have sponsors' names attached to them. Thus, there's the AT&T Cotton Bowl, the FedEx Orange Bowl, the Allstate Sugar Bowl, and the Rose Bowl Presented by CITI. Unlike the others, Rose Bowl officials—in an attempt to preserve that game's standing as "The Granddaddy of Them All"— refused to allow a sponsor to have first billing in its name. Conversely, the Peach Bowl completely lost its identity and was replaced by the Chick-fil-A Bowl; and the Fiesta Bowl is now the Tostitos Fiesta Bowl. Other named bowl game sponsors include Auto Zone, Capital One, GMAC, Little Caesar's, Outback, Papa John's, and Sheraton.

This trend in the sports world is by no means limited to football. According to published reports, an online casino paid one of the boxers in a recent middleweight championship match $100,000 to wear its logo emblazoned across the back of his boxing trunks—as well as its name printed on his back in large grease-painted letters. The fighter, a 5–2 underdog, reportedly bet the entire amount on himself, hitting the jackpot when he knocked out his opponent in the 12th round. *Who says advertising doesn't pay?*

## How Many Ads Do You See Each Day?

Try counting the number of ads you see in one day. Advertising is on sidewalks, on the beach, on cars, on signs, on clothing, in radio and TV commercials, and even *during* television shows and movies. It's on scrolling lighted signs at banks, grocery stores, schools, restaurants, auto dealerships, pharmacies—and even outside of churches.

Remember when a TV commercial break meant one or two advertising messages that lasted a total of 60 seconds, leaving you with barely enough time to run to the refrigerator or the bathroom? Now, you're hit with a dozen or more commercials in a row, giving you time, it seems, to eat dinner or take a long walk. Incidentally, have you noticed that commercials aired during the dinner hour seem to focus on various bodily functions—subjects that were once taboo in polite society, much less than on national television? It's enough to take away one's appetite completely.

The average American is subjected to more than 3,000 marketing messages daily; messages that are undoubtedly diluted in this overexposed world. But does this mean you should eliminate advertising from your marketing playbook? Absolutely *not!* You just have to find the appropriate vehicle for your product, service, and customers.

## Don't Waste Your Money! Test and Track

An essential rule is that any advertising you do needs to stand apart from your competition in terms of look, size, and message. Don't waste your advertising dollars by simply submitting your business card to a newspaper or magazine for exposure. You need results these days—and you need them in short order.

It's absolutely critical to test your headline, message, and ad size. Advertising executive David M. Ogilvy's advice: "The most important word in the vocabulary of advertising is *test*. If you pretest your product with consumers as well as your advertising, you will do well in the marketplace."

Indeed, advertising can be successful if done properly; that's why so many businesses continue to do it! But be sure to discern and track where your business is coming from, so that you can determine what advertising media are working for you. Purchase an 800 number, use a different number in each of your ads; or simply ask customers how they heard about you and track your findings. It is critical to determine whether your ads are having any measurable success; without it, there is no need to spend your time and money advertising.

How do you track the success of your marketing activities?

_____

_____

_____

_____

## The Three Keys to Successful Advertising

No matter what medium you use, new or traditional, there are three certainties for creating effective advertising.

1. Have a clear target for your product/service.
2. Research the demographics of the medium's audience to make sure it meets your intended audience.
3. Reach your audience with an impactful message requesting specific and direct action.

## A Grass Roots Approach to Reaching a Target Market

*Advertising Age* magazine selected car-sharing service company Zipcar as one of the hottest brands of 2009. An article by Kunur Patel that appeared in the November 16, 2009, issue of the magazine stated that the key to

Zipcar's success is finding innovative ways to reach customers. Zipcar's membership increased more than 40 percent in 2009, because the company focused their marketing directly on their target audience.

Zipcar is in more than 50 cities and college campuses in North America, as well as London. Their target is urbanites who live within a 10-minute walk from their cars. Zipcar was formed under the assumption that people who live in or near major cities with public transportation available should ditch their cars and instead engage in car sharing. These people can use public transportation, cycling, or walk to work. When they do need a car for a trip to the grocery store or visiting a friend in the suburbs, members can rent a Zipcar by the hour. The membership fee includes gas, maintenance, parking, and insurance. The cost to rent an average Zipcar is about $8.50 per hour, after a $50 annual membership fee.

Zipcar chairman and CEO Scott Griffith said in the article, "Even with today's highly targeted web, it's hard to target at that hyper-local level." To meet this challenge, Zipcar has hired marketing teams in each city to reach out to potential customers right where they live. Their strategy includes door hangers, bus shelter and subway posters, public relations, local promotions, partnerships with local businesses such as dry cleaners and coffee shops, and some local web ads. Zipcar's message appeals to potential members' lifestyles and questions the need to own a car in a big city. The company actually reports that 30 percent of its new members come directly from word of mouth. The key is to get the word out right where the potential customers live—and that's exactly what Zipcar did.

---

Where do your customers live? How can you reach them directly?

_____

_____

_____

_____

---

## Are Newspapers Dead? No!

Mark Twain once silenced rumors of his death with this note: "The report of my death was an exaggeration." The same might be said today of the "death" of the newspaper industry. Although the Age of Technology has led many newspapers all across America to close—and left others in serious financial straits—reports of the entire industry's demise are indeed an exaggeration.

In fact, newspaper advertising can be successful for locally owned businesses that target consumers in that same geographic area. Check each newspaper's circulation to see how well this might work for your brand. A paid-circulation paper will typically generate more sales because the readers have invited the medium into their homes, thereby indicating that your ad will be seen.

## Radio Advertising Brings Quick Exposure

Most small businesses have considered advertising in local newspapers and even the Yellow Pages, but traditionally only a few advertise on radio. However, local radio offers a quick and powerful way to reach a high percentage of people in a local marketplace.

Commercials can be created in a cost-efficient manner when you use one of the smaller radio stations to assist with production. Stations will usually offer in-house creative and production services—an extremely reasonable option for small businesses. Larger businesses should certainly use their advertising agencies to take the radio ad from concept to recording.

Pay close attention to the station or stations where you plan to advertise. Take the time to determine who you're trying to reach, what stations your target market is listening to, and during what time periods. Some products and services sell better than others on radio, so ask the local station for its demographic statistics. Request testimonials from other advertisers, and conduct your own research by listening to the stations to find out who's currently advertising on them.

You'll also need to determine what frequency of advertising will bring you results, which will depend on whether you're building a brand, selling a product or service, or promoting an event. The ideal is to get a message across at least three times in a "purchase cycle," which could be a week for a grocery store to a month or more for an automobile dealership. The theory here is that the first time will provide recognition; the second time will prompt the listener to possibly pay attention to the message; and the final time will solicit action. If an average listener hears 12 hours of radio a week, a grocery store will need to advertise its weekly sales items at least 30 to 40 times during that time period.

## Television and Cable

The major television networks—NBC, CBS, Fox, and ABC—distribute programming through local affiliates in more than 300 designated market areas (DMAs) across the country, some of which charge thousands of dollars for a 30-second spot. And in addition to the much larger cost, television advertising can actually be fairly inefficient for the target audience you're trying to reach. It may or may not prove to be a sound investment, depending on what you are selling, your objectives, and your call to action. In order to garner results, your TV ad has to motivate viewers to do something at that moment; otherwise, it will quickly leave their minds. You may build exposure for your product, service, or brand, but if immediate sales are your first objective, it is possible to both reach your target audience and reduce costs by purchasing cable spots. Local cable systems are able to preempt the spots feeding down from the network satellites and fill them with regional spots. These locally available spots, or "avails," offer advertisers a much narrower geographic distribution at a lower cost.

To achieve success in television advertising, you need to first define your target. Determine exactly whom you're trying to reach with your commercials, and look at the demographic data for your clients. Then match the cable network programming to your target, and schedule your commercials when your target audience is watching TV.

Second, you have to determine your geographic target. Some products simply will not prompt consumers to drive beyond a 60-mile radius of their homes. There are thousands of geographic zones across the country, and cable allows you to limit your advertising to the exact one that will work best for you.

## Infomercials

Infomercials help brands sell more than $4 billion products and services every year. These long-format television commercials—typically five minutes or longer—are also known as paid programming, and present a significant amount of information to viewers. These types of advertisements began appearing on television stations in the overnight hours as an alternative to signing off for the day. Today, most U.S. infomercials appear anytime throughout the day.

Although some members of the advertising industry view infomercials as second-rate campaigns, in general, they *work*. That's why they are on all the time! So whether you use the medium or not, the following elements are what make it so successful.

- *They build a comprehensive and convincing case*. Infomercials are designed to capture viewers' mindshare, inspire them to write down their phone number, dial it, and buy. And the only way that will happen is if the infomercial works as a complete stand-alone sales presentation. Most advertisements you see on TV focus on a core benefit of a product, whereas infomercials must cover *all* the features and benefits of a given product in order to gain results. The goal is to build a comprehensive and convincing case for buying by giving viewers all the information they need to make a purchasing decision. They explain every benefit, answer all objections, and then do it again.

- *They present testimonials to eliminate objections.* Infomercials prove the worthiness of their products by showing them in action and then presenting the results with real customers. The goal is to inspire you to act by taking all of your objections away.

- *They provide a strong and immediate call to action.* Infomercials make a specific offer. They don't give you many options or choices to customize; instead, they make the recommendation easy to understand. You essentially have only two choices: buy, or don't buy. And to get you to act right away, the offer is typically doubled, or accompanied by an additional free product. This special offer is meant to tip you over the edge and get you to decide on an impulse to buy immediately instead of putting it off.

## Too Good To Be True?

The P90X infomercial has created a cult following for an intense, 90-day workout system. The infomercial focuses on a workout that will get you from "flab to fit" in 90 days. Program creator Tony Horton tells the story of the product's background, shows everything that it takes to do the program, displays countless before-and-after photos, and presents real testimonials from people who have turned their bodies and lives around using the program. The entire infomercial has a persistent call to action to buy.

It's probably easy to think during a short-form advertisement, "Really? Three short months to turn my whole life around using an exercise system? I doubt it!" Viewers are likely to dismiss this quickly, and without much thought, move on with their lives. But this "too good to be true" objection is successfully conquered throughout the entire infomercial. User testimonials make the benefits clear, and the objections are systematically overcome. The risk has been reduced to nearly zero. After watching the infomercial, you feel like you have no choice but to buy. Now *that's* a successful commercial!

What can you do in your regular advertising and promotion that makes infomercials work? Here are four points.

1. Tell a story and show the product in action.
2. Layer it with powerful customer testimonials.
3. Have strong and continuous calls to action.
4. Overcome objections (again and again).

Would an infomercial be an option for your product or service? If so, what is your next step to put it into action?

## Take 15 and Get Your Clients Going Wild!
### A 15-Minute Client-Builder Exercise

Plan your advertising by first considering what you will sell, your message, testing and tracking techniques. Write out your plan for effective advertising.

## In Other Words

*Advertising says to people, "Here's what we've got. Here's what it will do for you. Here's how to get it."*

—*Leo Burnett*

## CHAPTER 16

# Direct Mail

## Simple Principles for Gaining Sales from Good Old-Fashioned Mail

*Direct mail is still a great way to get your company, service, or product in front of a completely new audience.*

We're living in the age of electronics. One look at the way you operate in your daily life makes this obvious. These days, it's commonplace to communicate virtually *everything* via e-mail. You send evites to those you want at your teleconferences, webinars, and even social gatherings. There's e-commerce and e-businesses that deal in e-money; and you keep in touch via instant messaging, online social networks, and videoconferencing. Even your schedules are updated and managed electronically. Soon filing cabinets, rolodexes, and datebooks will join the ever-growing list of "Things You Used to Use."

As these old ways of doing things start to gather dust, the same thought should be applied for "snail mail," right? After all, who actually bothers to stuff paper into envelopes, stamp them, and send them off anymore? *Savvy businesspeople, that's who!* In fact, more money is spent on direct mail advertising than on any other form of advertising. Why? Because, when it's done correctly, it *works*.

Though its more modern counterparts—like e-mail marketing, e-newsletters, social networks, search engine marketing, and so on—are growing in popularity, you shouldn't overlook direct mail as something that can get the job done. In fact, it's well worth your time and money to take advantage of this highly effective sales and marketing strategy.

## What Exactly Is Direct Mail?

Direct mail pieces can fall under a number of categories, from postcards to brochures to invitations to letters and so on. And they can be used to market most *anything*. In fact, direct mail creates one of the most intimate communications with customers of all advertising vehicles, because recipients can physically touch direct mail. People are reading content in a form that won't go away with the click of a mouse.

Remember, too, that unlike e-mail, recipients don't have to opt into your direct mail list, so you can send pieces to anyone. This is why direct mail is still a great way to get your company, service, or product in front of a completely new audience—and to cement your ongoing relationships with current and past clients as well.

### The Proof Is in the Numbers

Do you think your mailbox would be filled every day if direct mail *didn't* work? You receive on average 5 to 10 pieces of marketing material per day—something that simply would not be happening if companies felt they were throwing their money away. Ken Erdman, the late chairman of PacRim Marketing Group (a Honolulu-based international marketing communications and sales promotion firm) makes the case well: "Contrary to a long-popular image of direct mail as unwanted mail, most people—and particularly businesspeople—not only read advertising mail but act on it." Erdman said, "Scientific opinion research supports these facts, and more importantly, the sales and service dollar figures generated by direct mail attest to its effectiveness. Nobody likes an empty mailbox."

In fact, global consulting firm the Winterberry Group expects direct mail in the United States to continue growing at a rate of 5 percent a year until at least 2011. By that point, it will hit $72.3 billion. And what about customer satisfaction? Research also found that 87 percent of consumers are satisfied with the goods and services they purchase as a result of receiving direct mail.

Clearly, it's a viable strategy, and it may also be the oldest marketing tool on the planet, a further testament to its effectiveness.

According to a spokesman for the New York University Center for Direct Marketing, "The roots of direct mail go back thousands of years and include messages written in hieroglyphics on papyrus and fabric sent throughout the Egyptian kingdom about 3000 BC."

Now, 5,000 years later, there is debate as to whether direct mail has outlived its usefulness. Many people have negative impressions of this medium. Their complaints range from "direct mail is a waste of money" to "I never read *my* junk mail, so I'm sure no one is reading the mail *I* send." But those impressions don't prove to be correct.

Although direct mail is not an exact science, response rates to direct mailings are generally around 0.4 percent to 2 percent (a 5 percent response rate would be quite noteworthy). Although these rates might initially seem low, think about it: for every 100 postcards or letters you send out, you will probably get one response. And if you're selling, say, a phone service or insurance policies, then the cost of printing and sending those hundred mailings will be *more* than offset by the revenue you're likely to pull in from the one person who says "Tell me more!" or "I'll take it!"

### An 819 Percent Return on Investment? Really?!

Joan & Ed's Deli in Natick, Massachusetts, received an 11 percent response rate by offering $3 off the next order of $20 or more (cash sales only). The mailer featured a picture of the business owners on the front with copy that called out "times are tough . . . save money by eating at Joan & Ed's" (see Figure 16.1). This family-owned restaurant has been in business for more than 32 years, and their personal service and owners' personalities have always been important to their customers. So that's what they featured.

The campaign cost $649.80, and 188 people took the deli up on the offer. Total revenue generated was $5,970.42, and even after subtracting the cost of the $3 per order offer, the final revenue was still $5,406.42!

### The Formula for Direct Mail Success

According to Tom Egelhoff, direct mail expert and author of the book *How to Market, Advertise, and Promote Your Business or Service in Your Own Backyard* (John Wiley & Sons, Inc., 2008), in order to have an effective campaign, you first need to know what you want. If you are looking for a particular amount of new revenue, you have to send out a certain number of mailing pieces to realize your goal. Test out the following formula on your next mailing.

Figure 16.1   Joan & Ed's Deli Postcard

*Source:* Joan & Ed's Deli.

# A Simple Direct Mail Formula

1. Revenue goal that you want your mailing to produce.

   _____

2. Average sale amount of product/service.

   _____

3. Your closing ratio (for example, if 100 customers are interested in the product and 50 end up buying it, your closing ratio is 50 percent).

   _____

4. Estimate your mailing response rate. (Most direct mail campaigns produce a 0.25 percent to 2.5 percent response.)

   _____

Enter your numbers in the calculation:
Avg. Sale _____ × Close Ratio _____ × Response Rate _____ = _____/Revenue Goal _____ = # to mail
$75 × 50 percent × 1 percent = 0.25 divided into $10,000 = 26,666 pieces

---

Let's suppose that you can improve your response rate just 1 percent with a better offer. In that case, you would only need to mail 13,333 pieces. If you mailed out postcards at 28¢ per card, you'll save $3,733.24 in postage—to achieve the same $10,000 in revenue!

It seems like common sense, but it's so easy to lose money in a direct mail campaign if you haven't properly considered this formula. And when it comes to direct mail, small towns have a definite advantage over large cities. First, the list is usually smaller. For example, your customer base in a town of 25,000 may only be 10 percent (2,500 people). Mailing postcards to 2,500 potential customers—even at full first class postcard postage of 28¢—is $700. If you mail to this group once a quarter or season (four times a year), you are looking at postage costs of $233.33 per month. And, if addressed properly, the post office will charge considerably less through their bulk mail program.

**A word of caution:** Be aware that individuals have the right to obtain a Prohibitory Order, which prevents nongovernmental organizations from sending unsolicited mail. Be diligent about removing these individuals' information from your lists, whether that list was purchased or compiled by you. Failure to do so is considered a criminal offense in the United States.

## Simple May Be Better!

Mosaic Hair Studio (www.mosaichairstudio.com) is a small boutique salon near downtown Orlando, owned and operated by husband-and-wife team Michael and Kiri Van den Abbeel. For the last six years, the couple has mailed a monthly direct mail letter to all residents new to the area (based on zip code and mortgage amount). The letter welcomes them to the area, gives them some information about the hair studio, and offers a $20 discount on any service in the salon. It also includes several client testimonials about the quality of service at Mosaic (see Figure 16.2). The envelope is handwritten, and the Van den Abbeels use first class stamps. The list—sourced from Newpros Data for $52.75 per month—provides about 100 to 150 names per month (they were getting as many as 400 names during the housing boom). Mosaic's monthly expense for this campaign averages $115, and they return at least $250 in sales each month with a majority of new clients becoming their regular clients. "This is the only marketing our salon has ever done," said Michael. "It consistently has returned anywhere from 2 percent to 6 percent with an overall average of 3.5 percent per month." A real and simple success!

## The Elements of Direct Mail Success

Simply inserting your company's brochure in an envelope and sending it off—or tossing some postcards you have left over from last year in the mail—is not an effective way to use direct mail. Experts in this area say that 40 percent of a campaign's effectiveness is driven by the mailing list, 40 percent by the offer, and 20 percent by the creative package. And there are many factors within those components that attribute to a successful direct mail campaign. Let's take a look at what these are.

### The Right Design

Everyone knows how important first impressions are. Your direct mail piece must compete for your recipient's attention with everything else in his or her mailbox. And if it's not compelling enough, it'll end up in the garbage, unopened and unread. Ideally, the design of your piece will spark

**"You're never too old to look younger"** –*Mae West*

Dear New Neighbor!

You probably miss your favorite salon and trusted stylist from the town you just moved from, and finding a new stylist may seem like an unpleasant or even a frightful and daunting task. We'd certainly like to make that easier for you... and to make it a very pleasant experience.

My name is Mike Van den Abbeel from Mosaic Hair Studio, and my wife Kiri and I understand the importance of fabulous hair to your overall attitude and appearance. We specialize in eliminating unflattering, does-nothing-for-you hair. With extensive training in London, New York, Chicago and Miami, plus a full range of hair services, we can offer you a trendy, confident new look.

Right now though, we just want to welcome you to the neighborhood. As a welcome gift, bring in this letter and use it as a $20 savings certificate that can be applied towards any services at our salon. Plus, with absolutely no obligation, you'll be treated to a completely free scalp massage - who needs it more than a person who has just moved?

Please feel free to drop in and have a glass of wine or cup of coffee with us, or call us at Mosaic Hair Studio if there is anything we can do for you. If you are interested in learning a little more about us before you call, go ahead and visit our website at www.mosaichairstudio.com. We look forward to becoming your next favorite salon and stylists.

Sincerely,

Mike Van den Abbeel     Kiri

Mosaic Hair Studio

**Mosaic Hair Studio**
537 Virginia Drive • Orlando, Florida 32803
(407) 896-3241
mosaichairstuido@hotmail.com
www.mosaichairstudio.com

**Figure 16.2   Mosaic Hair Studio New Move Letter**
*Source*: Mosaic Hair Studio.

the recipient's curiosity to investigate further. But don't go overboard—if your direct mail looks like junk to you, it will look like junk to the recipient. Consider using bright color, pictures of real people using your product or service, and bold headlines. Also, use different type styles such as bold, underline, and ALL CAPITAL letters to draw your reader's eye to key messages. And make sure your offer, call to action, and response date are clearly visible.

Another strategy is to use odd-sized envelopes or packaging to pique the recipient's curiosity. You want to do whatever you can to get the envelope opened and your message read. You can also take the headline from your direct mail letter and duplicate it on the front of the envelope, which entices the reader to open and read on. If the outer envelope doesn't convey importance, the mail will likely be thrown away without ever being opened. Reasons that are compelling to get them a reader to your message can include an offer and/or benefit message, and if you're mailing to current clients, your logo may be enough to get them to open the envelope.

*Size matters*, too. Use a large postcard! There's no envelope that has to be stuffed with a letter, the recipient has nothing to open, and your message is right in front of the reader. Try this for an inexpensive yet response-generating design. It really works!

---

What design elements will you use to get your message to stick out?

_____

_____

_____

_____

---

## The Right Message

Direct mail should clearly state what benefit(s) the reader will enjoy by taking the requested action. Again—people don't buy features, they buy benefits and results. You are not buying a couch for your house—you are buying a plush, beautiful, soft, and stunning piece of furniture, and the ability to relax and sit comfortably.

Include the following in your powerful message:

- *Benefits*. Your message should communicate benefits—not features! Every word needs to show the reader "WIIFM"—What's In It For Me. For example, the main enticement for action isn't the fact that the premium movie channel you're offering customers is available in high-definition. Buyers want to know that they'll have 24/7 access to a wide variety of the latest releases, all with theater-quality presentation. A benefit's statement will imply its features.

- *A powerful headline*. In order to have any chance at getting your prospects to read on and take action, you have to grab their interest from the beginning.

- *The first paragraph of a letter's copy must do the majority of the selling work.* Strive to keep all of your copy fast-paced and exciting, even when imparting technical details. You don't want to lose the reader's interest midway through.

- *Testimonial quotes from satisfied clients.* This is an excellent way for you to prove that you have delivered the results you claim for others. Testimonials should specifically state how your product or service solved the problem or changed the life of your satisfied client.

- *Include information on your company's track record and trustworthiness.* You should assure your potential buyers that your company has high customer satisfaction rates and that you can be trusted to provide what you say you will—especially if your aim is to directly sell a product. Even on a postcard, there's room to say something like, "America's trusted source for hand-crafted fine jewelry since 1924!"

- *A money-back guarantee or warranty.* Take away the fear of spending money, and clients won't be as leery of buying something sight unseen.

- *Make an offer with a specific call to action.* The goal isn't to make the recipient think it would be "nice" to have what you're offering; it's to convince him or her that it's a *necessity*—one that must be acquired *right now*.

## Your Offer and Call to Action

Make sure that your direct mail pieces include a clear and specific call to action. If your offer isn't specific, valuable, and useful enough, even the most masterful copy in the world won't get you the results you want. Your audience needs to feel that they are part of a select group that's been chosen to receive a special offer or value, and they need to be convinced after they put your piece down that the sooner they respond to your offer, the better.

How can you ensure that you've included an effective call to action? There are a few ways to tell:

- *Include a specific offer.* Direct mail is not a good tool for image advertising, but it's an effective vehicle for direct response. Give your readers something to respond to immediately; for example, offer a free, 30-minute, first-time consultation. Provide 25 percent off if they order by a specific date, or invite them to RSVP to an event.

Enclose a "two for one" coupon good for a discount if used within 30 days, or a CD with a trial version of your program.

- *Add a sense of urgency to your direct mail.* Establish a deadline for the offer so that action is taken. For example:
  - "Register by June 15 to receive a $100 discount on membership."
  - "This sale ends on August 1."
  - "Receive $20 off if you're one of the first 100 people to respond to this."

- *Offer a two-step approach.* The two-step approach provides the reader with the ability to take an initial "baby step" to find out more information about your company before you try to sell them. The goal here is to get people to respond—but maybe not buy just yet. Entice them with a free report or free event. This approach creates a new mailing list of people who are responders—and a much warmer audience for your next campaign.

- *"Buy One, Get One Free" works better than "50 Percent Off."* Also, fear of loss is more powerful than expectation of gain. So phrases like, "Limited Time Offer," "Respond Now," or "Don't Miss Out On Big Savings" usually draw more customers in.

- *Repeat it!* Generally speaking, a single-page direct mail letter might have the call to action listed three times: in the middle of the letter, in the last paragraph, and in the postscript.

What's your offer?

_____

_____

_____

_____

## The Right Target

Who makes up your customer base? What are the demographics of your most frequent clients? What other kinds of customers would you like to reach? Getting specific about those to whom you will mail is critical for any direct mail campaign success. The best design and message is invisible unless you're presenting it to the right audience.

If you expand beyond your current in-house clients, pick a list carefully. It's all too easy to end up with names outside your target market. Use a list company with a reputation for delivering accurate names that can be sorted based on the targeting information that's important to you. You can pursue customers based on a variety of factors like incomes, net worth, specific hobbies or interests, marital status, whether there are children, and more. And spend the extra time up front to make sure that your lists, whether bought or self-created, are as current as possible. They should be updated before each mailing to ensure that the widest range of *viable* customers is being targeted.

What is your target audience for your mailing?

_____

_____

_____

_____

## The Right Response Vehicle

Make it simple for your future customers to engage your services, order your product, or get in touch to learn more. Just as different products and services require distinct kinds of presentation, they also require different response vehicles. These might include a direct mail reply device such as a postage-paid, addressed envelope; an 800 number; an online order form; or a special web site for the offer. Whatever you decide to do, make the transactional details as simple as possible to navigate, and the contact information—for you or your company—located in multiple spots and easy to find.

What response vehicle(s) will you have?

_____

_____

_____

_____

## The Right Strategy—Test It!

After you purchase a list of prospective clients—but before you put in a large print order—make sure that an internal test audience gives your direct mailing piece's design, message, urgency, and offer a thumbs-up. Leave time to incorporate feedback, and you'll be sure to get the most for your money.

Test the value of the list you've purchased by doing a mailing to a portion of it. For example, if you acquire 10,000 names, select 1,000 or 1,500 at random and mail to them, or send different offers to different segments of the list. By testing various combinations of names and offers one at a time, you can determine which package and offer are most effective without incurring the expense of rolling out a mailing to the entire list.

Before you rush into a test, write down the answers to a few basic questions:

- Why am I testing?
- What are my objectives?
- What questions do I want answered?
- What will I measure with this test?
- How much time do I have for a test?
- What is my budget for testing?

How will you test your strategy?

_____

_____

_____

_____

## Measure Your Responses

One of the great benefits of direct mail is the ability it gives you to obtain and measure responses. You can establish accurate measurement tools such as promotion codes and/or coupons without which it is sometimes difficult to determine if your efforts were successful. And the more data you can track, the better.

*Keep detailed reports on the following data:*

1. Number of pieces mailed
2. Number of responses you received
3. Response source
4. Conversion percentage
5. Income those responses generate
6. Average order
7. Percentage response
8. Cost per order or cost per response
9. Net profit
10. Returns and bad debt

---

## Take 15 and Get Your Clients Going Wild!
### A 15-Minute Client-Builder Exercise

Plan your next direct mail campaign using the five key elements: Design, Message, Target, Response Vehicle, and Strategy Test. When will you start? What are your objectives?

_____

_____

_____

_____

# Events and Seminars

## Creating Buzz and Sales Through Group Presentations

There's a good chance that the thought of events and seminars conjures up some negative imagery for you—memories of stale conference rooms, boring speakers who drone on and on, or being harassed to sign on the dotted line at an overcrowded trade show. If previous experiences have left a bad taste in your mouth, then chances are you aren't jumping at the opportunity to spend your own company's most precious resources—time and money—to host one of your own.

But the truth is that when they're planned well, events and seminars can be effective means of connecting, networking, marketing, and promoting your business. The key is to know how to do them right.

In addition, clients and prospects often need to be reassured that you operate a credible, healthy business. When you host an event—especially one operated in conjunction with other companies, community groups, and the media—people will see your company as trustworthy. Since public events are open to public scrutiny, people generally feel that any company willing to be so open and upfront must be confident about what it has to offer.

An event doesn't have to be large to accomplish your goal, whether it's to educate, enhance name recognition, build relationships, or generate sales. Great events come in all shapes and sizes; so read on for some fresh ideas (and some oldies-but-goodies) to help get your first big event off the ground.

## Get Eventful

There are countless events to use to generate buzz about your business. The key is to find the right kinds for you—those that will keep you inspired, impress your clients, and create loyal employees. Naturally, you can be as creative as you like, but to help get you started, here are a few popular options.

### Web-Based Events

Technology has certainly changed the way you do business, and events are no exception. Today's high-tech event options allow you to play host to a number of clients or other stakeholders without ever leaving your office. Read on to see how to get onboard with getting online.

> *Host a webinar.* Hosting an online educational event, workshop, or seminar can attract new and old clients by providing them with a solution to a potential problem, giving answers to questions they may have, and building your own credibility. In the end, if you supply the information or help they're looking for, they'll be encouraged to buy your product or use your service. As an added bonus, webinars can be money-making endeavors; remember to include offers for your products or services either during the webinar or as part of your call to action at the end.
>
> > **Bonus Tip:** Always record your webinars. This gives those who couldn't make the original webinar the opportunity to take part on their own time, whenever they're available. You might even consider offering webinars that received particularly great feedback as downloadable for a price after the original live event.
>
> *Podcast yourself.* If you have some great ideas to share with your clients, but you aren't exactly sure how to make the connection, then a podcast may be the silver bullet you've been awaiting. Hosting a regular podcast is like having an online version of your own prerecorded radio or television show available for all to hear (or see) via cyberspace.
>
> Consider recording a weekly or monthly series to which your clients, employees, and other colleagues can subscribe. Keep your topics relevant, current, and interesting. After all, you want to make sure your listeners (or viewers) keep coming back for more.

*Hold an online product demonstration.* Product demonstrations are a great way to keep clients (and potential customers) in the loop on the latest and greatest innovations that your company has to offer. But if your client base is national or international, then traveling from place to place for a product demonstration just isn't cost-effective or feasible.

This is where the Web comes in: Holding a live product demonstration online is a great way for clients to connect with you and your company, without the added cost and hassle involved with travel. For added efficiency, you can record these sessions and post them on your web site or social networking sites, like Twitter and Facebook, so that clients or potential clients who may have missed the live demonstration still have the opportunity to log on and see what you have to offer.

List the web-based events you will host.

_____
_____
_____
_____

## Networking Events

All networking events are not created equal. You don't have to limit your efforts in this area to trade shows, conference rooms, or whomever you're sitting next to on your flight. Read on for some networking events that allow you to get the job done—and have a little fun, too.

*Host a happy hour.* Who doesn't love happy hour? Make arrangements at a local watering hole to host your own, and invite people in your network and ask them to bring a friend. The lure of half-priced drinks and the chance to meet like-minded peers is difficult for most people to turn down. If you find that you draw a fairly large crowd, consider making it a quarterly or monthly event.

*Hold an open house.* Open houses are a great way to reconnect with your current clients while also allowing you to establish ties with your business and community neighbors. Open your doors to clients and their families, and extend that invitation to residents of the surrounding community. Consider serving refreshments, having door prizes or a raffle, and offering fun activities for people to do. Sometimes all it takes to make that next great connection is to get people in the door—and an open house is a great way to do just that!

*Include a celebrity appearance.* Nothing draws a crowd quite like a celebrity. Don't worry—your event's personality doesn't have to be a Hollywood A-lister. Consider asking someone who is well known within your particular field or area of interest, or ask a local celebrity or perhaps a successful entrepreneur in your town or elected official. Just remember to advertise, advertise, advertise! Having a well-known name attached to your event is a surefire way to garner interest and boost attendance numbers.

*Have a working luncheon.* Many times all it takes to generate great conversation is great food. Consider hosting a luncheon that doubles as a networking opportunity. Whether you cater it in-house or rent out a room at a local restaurant, you want to make sure you are in an environment that is conducive to conversation (a loud, open restaurant is probably not the best idea) and that you spend some time speaking to everyone in attendance. You never know—this year's most profitable connection just might be made over dessert!

*Tee off.* Thinking outside the proverbial networking box is an effective way to create a different kind of event—one that people will actually *want* to attend. And sometimes that means networking, well, outside. Consider the demographic of clients, potential clients, and colleagues with whom you want to network, and think of an activity they'd enjoy. It may mean a day on the golf course, an afternoon at the spa, or even a picnic in a local park. There's no rule that says you can't network and do fun activities at the same time. And getting people involved in something they enjoy prompts them to let their guard down, and, in turn, makes networking a little easier and much more successful.

List the networking events you will host.

_____

_____

_____

_____

## Client-Focused Events

Although events are a great way to make new connections and bring in new business, you certainly don't want to forget the customers you already have! Hosting client-focused events is a great way to stay connected to your current customers and to keep them coming back for more.

> *Hold a weekend workshop.* Solution-based workshops and events generate sales with shorter lead times. For example, hosting a workshop entitled, "How to Avoid Common Mistakes When Selling Your House," will obviously attract attendees who are looking for solutions to problems or concerns they currently have. This provides a highly targeted group. Just like a cooking class or tile-laying demonstration, people will appreciate the opportunity to improve their skill-set by taking your class at a time when they can fit it into their own busy schedules.
>
> *Hold client-appreciation events.* These kinds of events help you build stronger relationships with your current clients in a day and age when loyalty is increasingly hard to come by. Depending on your business and proximity to your clients, you could host a picnic or a client-appreciation dinner. You could also conduct special workshops that focus on a timely matter in your industry, a new product, or upgraded technology.

A client orientation is another way to build relationships. Invite all the new clients you've acquired in the previous month or quarter to a scheduled orientation. This gives them the opportunity to ask questions, get to know your staff, find out more about the products or services they purchased, network with other clients—and enjoy the refreshments you provide. Automobile dealers, chiropractors, financial advisors, and many other business and professional people often do this for new customers and clients. It's an excellent way to build goodwill.

---

List the client events you will host.

_____

_____

_____

_____

---

## Traditional Events

If you're more of a traditionalist, then you may want to consider trying out some of the following tried-and-true event ideas. As always, feel free to spice them up a bit with your own creative ideas and unique twists.

*If in retail, hold a sales event.* If you work in retail and you want to increase traffic and attract attention, then there's nothing more effective than having a sale. No matter the economic climate, people are always looking for a bargain, and offering them one is a great way to get them in your door. You can host a sale annually, seasonally, or just because; whatever the reason, make sure you get the word out and that your staff is prepared to handle the extra foot-traffic a sale can bring.

*Or host an in-store promotion.* An important thing to remember is that a promotion doesn't necessarily mean having a sale. There are other creative ways to draw customers that don't involve slashing prices. What activities or special events can you can do right in your store that will draw customers and generate interest in your products? For example—if you own a vineyard or a store that sells wine, then host a wine-tasting. If your store sells home goods, then hold a workshop on how to create the perfect table setting, or have a chef come in for a live demonstration. Whatever you choose, make sure that the event showcases your products and services in a way that customers won't soon forget.

*Present at a trade show.* The trick at trade shows is to stand out from every Tom, Dick, and Mary that also happens to be there. Make sure that your booth is on prime trade show real estate—on the end of an aisle, near the food court, or at the entrance to the show room. When setting up your booth, think of it as a retail store, and design the space in a way that is appealing to the eye and that will draw people in. Use lots of signage so that people are clear on who you are and what you represent.

*If you have staff with you, train them to be friendly and knowledgeable so they will be prepared for any questions from potential customers.* Remember that giving something away (that is emblazoned with your company logo, of course) is always a crowd favorite. Consider holding mini-seminars or product demonstrations in your booth, and make sure that any products you have on display are fully operational before you put them out for all to see.

*Form a strategic alliance.* "Joining forces" informally or formally with a partner allows you to greatly increase your chances of success and ultimately realize greater profits. Hosting a joint sidewalk sale is one great way for two businesses to partner with one another in hopes of mutual success. For example, a pet store and a grooming salon team up. The pet store can host a sidewalk sale outside of the grooming shop, while the groomer offers special discounts on the same day.

This allows two different businesses that share a similar clientele to profit from one event.

*Host an annual party.* Whether you are celebrating the nation's independence on July 4 or sharing a glass of eggnog in December, you should make your party a yearly event. Keeping it consistent makes it something your clients will expect (and look forward to), which means that they've already cleared their calendars in anticipation and will be more likely to attend. Whatever you do, make sure the party you throw is a good one. The best way to ensure that people keep coming back is to make it the can't-miss event of the year!

*Schedule a book signing.* If you've written a book, the obvious choice of event for you is to do a book signing. And no, you don't need to go to the trouble of scheduling a cross-country book tour. But if you are planning to travel, call bookstores in the cities that you're visiting to see if they would be interested in letting you arrange a book signing. You should also place calls to your local stores. When you are scheduling your local signings, consider sticking with one of your town's independent book stores—it's another great way to create a strategic alliance and support your community!

---

List the traditional-type events you will host.

_____

_____

_____

_____

---

## Give Back: Community Events

Not only is giving back the right thing to do—as well as a great morale booster—it's also a great way to get involved with your community and to get your name out there. But remember: You absolutely *must* have your heart in the cause. If you are just using these events for your own benefit, people will notice and it won't be any good for you or your company's reputation. That said—here are some ideas for ways that you can give back.

*Hold a fundraiser for a local charity.* No matter where you live, I guarantee that there are local charities and other organizations that could use your help. Host a dinner, a silent auction, or a "fun run" to raise money and awareness for the cause of your choice. You'll make some great lo-cal connections, get your name out there, and you'll be servicing a dire need in your community. In other words, it's a win-win.

*Volunteer your entire company for a cause.* Don't just stop at putting your company's name behind a great cause, get your employees in on the action, too. For example, volunteer for a Habitat for Humanity Day, or spend an afternoon serving lunch at a local soup kitchen.

*Be a good sport.* Sponsor a local sports team. Whether it's the recrea-tional department's little league team or the local high school football players, they will appreciate your help in buying things like equipment and jerseys. Offer to mentor or tutor players, if needed; and certainly show your support by having your colleagues attend a few games to cheer them on. As thanks for your efforts, most rec league teams will put your company's name somewhere on their jersey, and schools will often put up a sign or banner from your company on their home field.

*Adopt a classroom.* Adopt a class at a local school and help them throughout the year by purchasing school supplies, volunteering to tu-tor, and so forth. Then, host a big party at the end of the year for stu-dents and their families.

---

List the community events you will host.

_____

_____

_____

_____

---

## Employee-Focused Events

Most of your events will be client-centric. After all, the success of your business hangs on your ability to attract new customers, and keep the ones you've got happy. But don't forget about your employees! They are the bread and butter of your organization, and without them, you lose an integral part of what makes your company a success. After all, happy employees = happy clients!

*Hold motivational meetings.* Everybody needs a little encouragement once in awhile, and your employees are no exception. Every now and then, gather the troops for a motivational meeting. Remind them what your company is all about, what you are working toward, and how they are an important part of that equation. Show them how their hard work is being translated into results. Sometimes all it takes is a little break from the daily grind to renew their spirits and keep them motivated.

*Celebrate employee and company achievements.* There are many unsung heroes among workforces, and it's high time that they are recognized. Make a point to observe the great achievements your employees make. Nobody is saying that you have to give out a trophy every time someone makes a sale, but it won't hurt to take five minutes out of the workday to let everyone else know what a great job someone is doing.

And if your company has a particularly good month or quarter, celebrate! Cater in a lunch one day, or let everyone leave a little early on a Friday afternoon. It doesn't have to be an expensive blowout of a party. Simply taking the time to focus on the positive aspects of the job will keep employees motivated and happy.

*Today is (someone's) birthday.* Celebrating employee birthdays is a great way to show your employees that you care. Use these as an opportunity to celebrate your staff members. Give your employees the chance to be in the spotlight on their birthdays, and highlight their contributions to the company and their redeeming attributes. Sharing a slice of cake in the conference room is a great way to connect with your employees; and they will appreciate the camaraderie and the chance to be recognized.

*Get out of the office.* Sometimes a change of scenery can be a great way to rejuvenate your employees. Holding an out-of-the-office event every couple of months or so gives everyone at your organization an opportunity to actually have some fun together. This can also be a great way to refill their tanks when they need it most. Go on a company day trip or weekend retreat. Ask employees to meet at a local park for a catered lunch and afternoon of fun. Or, if you are feeling really creative, divide your employees into teams and send them around your city or town on a scavenger hunt. It is a great team-building exercise that usually reminds employees that they actually *enjoy* being around one another.

List the employee events you will host.

_____

_____

_____

_____

## Making Meaningful Connections at Events

*Have a plan of action before you go.* Social events can be nerve-wracking. So instead of dreading the big event, formulate a plan of action ahead of time that will help you make the most of them. Doing so will ensure that you make all the right connections, and it will help to alleviate any pre-party social anxiety you may have.

*Let them do the talking. (You ask the questions!).* There's nothing worse than coming away from a great networking opportunity realizing that you didn't capitalize on the situation. As you work the crowds, be sure to have more in your arsenal than small talk. Come up with a list of questions to use on your new acquaintances. Here are a few icebreakers to get the ball rolling:

- Where did you grow up? Do you still have family there?
- How are your kids? What are they up to?
- What do you think about . . . ? (Complete this question with something from current events, your town or city's local news, or a recent event in your industry. Remember, it is always a good idea to avoid topics that can lead to contentious conversations, such as religion and politics.)

    Once the conversation is flowing freely, then you can move on to more in-depth business questions:

- What's the best thing that has happened to your business this year?
- What's one thing you've done that has really changed your career?
- What will you never do again in business?
- What's your biggest challenge?
- What makes a good client for you?
- What do you find is the most effective way to keep a client happy?

*Be prepared to pitch yourself in only 15 seconds.* You clearly have many qualifications and experience—so much that you could probably go on for *hours* about yourself. But the hard reality is that no one (except possibly your mother) wants to hear that much about your accomplishments. When meeting new people, you should resist the urge to give a 10-minute introduction of yourself. Instead, prepare a short, 15-second elevator pitch that hits on your career high points and top skills. Consider what's unique about what you have done and what will stand out in a room full of people who are also talking about themselves—and think about what will make the people you speak with remember you at the end of the night.

*The party may end, but your connection shouldn't.* Spend 10 minutes cementing your interactions by creating a database that allows you to keep track of all the connections you've made. Include reminders to yourself of interesting or remarkable things that people said or that you learned so that you won't forget them and can refer back to them in later conversations. And be sure to use social media to keep in touch.

## Get the Word Out

You can plan all you want, but if no one attends your event—it is worthless. Here's how to promote your next event and to ensure a great turnout and lots of positive attention for you and your company.

*Create a one-of-a-kind invite.* Design unique invitations that your guests will not be able to resist opening. Think of them as a direct mail marketing piece for your event. Emphasize to your invitees that they are your VIPs and one of only a small number of people being invited to your exclusive event. Depending on your budget, you may even want to include a T-shirt branded with the event name, date, and your company logo—or some other kind of promotional item to make it especially easy to remember.

*Make the most of social networking sites.* Create an events page on Facebook where invitees can RSVP and find information about the event. As the big day gets closer, tweet about what you have planned and send pictures of the set up; and keep tweeting during the event. Send more pictures, and encourage other attendees to do the same.

*Create an event-specific web site.* Set up an easy-to-navigate web site or web page on your company site that includes information about the event. This provides you with a great way to keep people informed of any updates, changes, or news that they may need to know about your event, and will also allow you to avoid spending the days leading up to your event fielding phone calls and e-mails with questions about the who, what, where, and when's. Remember to be sure to include a page or section that allows people to easily register/RSVP for the event.

*Send out an e-blast.* Create a well-designed e-blast that includes information about the event and how it will benefit those who attend. Send it out well in advance, and then send out another shortened version as a reminder once the event is closer.

*Remember, timing matters.* It's important that you not send out your promotional materials too soon or too late. Most people have busy lives and schedules that are already jam-packed, so letting them know about an event just one week in advance is a bad idea. Give attendees as much notice as possible. Start getting the word out as soon as you have a confirmed date, location, and time. If some attendees will have to travel to the event, allow plenty of time for them to make travel plans so that they can get good rates on airline tickets and hotels.

Coordinate your efforts so that those invited to the event first hear about it a few weeks before the scheduled date and then continue to get little reminders—either via your e-blast, social networking efforts, or web site—as the date approaches.

## Avoid a Party Foul

When it comes to events, there are a few simple dos and don'ts that can make yours a success (and help you avoid a major party foul!). Read on for what you should *and* shouldn't do at your next big gig.

Do *make time for an important event.* "I'm too busy" is not a valid excuse for not holding events that are potentially beneficial to client and employee relationships. If you are worried about how much time the planning will take, start small by hosting an employee luncheon or a strictly online event such as a webinar. Before you pass up these great opportunities, remember that even a small event can go a long way in improving your business.

Don't *play hardball.* One quick and effective way to destroy whatever goodwill your event may have otherwise generated is to try and sell your attendees anything. Giving them promotional materials as they leave is okay, but mentioning that you have products available "for their convenience," and that you take checks or credit cards, is the kiss of death.

Do *have a Plan B.* You've rented a meeting room that's set up for an audience of 50, and 150 people show up. If you haven't arranged for extra chairs, or a larger backup room, or enough refreshments for everyone, then all your hard work and expense in planning the event will have largely been wasted.

Do *get organized early on.* Checklists and an organized timeline can help you manage the details of events that help others—events that can be cost-effective, efficient tools for promoting your business, and building client loyalty.

Do *ask yourself—and then ask again—will this really help my customers?* Don't just put on an event for the sake of having it. If you aren't offering something of value to your customers—a networking opportunity, some type of training or information, or another valuable service—then it probably isn't worth your time or your money. Keep in mind that if your event attendees don't come away with something of value, then they won't waste *their* time attending again. Remember, your event speaks volumes to the quality of your company. If it lacks substance, customers may begin to question your product and services as well.

Don't *forget to collect information from participants.* A great way to figure out the demographics of your event attendees is to get to know them a little better. Find ways to collect information from participants through surveys and comment cards. Ask where they are from, why they attended, what industry they work in, and so forth. Find out what they liked and didn't like; and don't forget to ask for complete contact info for follow up. Having this information on hand will be a great resource for you when planning your next event, and will make it much easier to build on the connections you've made.

Don't *miss out on photo ops.* It's not only a great way to document an event, but people will feel special when you ask to have your picture taken with them. These pictures will also be useful later on when you want to show others how the event went via your Facebook, Twitter, e-newsletter, and so forth.

Do *film the event.* If you are speaking at the event, having a video of it can be a great way to pitch yourself for future speaking gigs. You can also post the clips on your web site to promote any future events you may organize.

Don't *try to do it all alone.* Putting on an event can be a lot of hard work—it involves many details, organizing, and planning. Trying to take on the endeavor on your own can be a huge mistake. Hire some help if you can, and don't be afraid to delegate or outsource when possible.

## The After Party: What to Do Once Your Event Is Over

*Follow up with connections.* After your event, think about the connections you made. Review any business cards or other contact information you collected, and take some time to reach out to each person individually. When you do so, recall an anecdote from your conversation, or a personal interest you may have discussed with that person. It will show that you were paying attention and that you truly value the link you established.

*Do what you said you would do.* Don't get so caught up in the excitement of your event that you start making promises you won't be able to keep when it's all over. If you don't think you can stick to a certain price, don't offer it. If you know you are already booked in the month of March, then don't tell someone you will come to their event during that time. Failing to follow through can cost you your credibility—and that can be a serious blunder when it comes to business.

*Start planning for next year.* Don't wait six months before you start planning next year's event—start immediately! Make some headway while this year's event is still fresh on your mind and you remember all the things that worked great, as well as the things that were less than stellar. You'll lock into better rates on things like catering and rentals if you book far enough in advance; and you'll save yourself a lot of stress as the event draws near.

## Speak Up

Great communicators are able to command respect, convey their ideas more quickly, and often, close more sales. They're also the ones who have developed a sense of a personal connection with those they may have never—nor will ever—personally meet. The truth is that the individuals who can speak effectively are more likely to advance through business, end up running many of the largest companies in the world, and become political leaders.

*Getting started.* Consider any organizations, conferences, or events that would make sense for you and your particular industry, and book yourself as a speaker at those events. Research on both the local and national level, and begin pitching yourself right away. The more speaking you do, the more you will book, and you will begin to see that you will become a celebrity of sorts as a keynote speaker. Speaking events are great opportunities for gaining new contacts and building your business.

A great way to get started with your speaking career is to think local. Try to book yourself at events in your state or region. You'll build momentum by obtaining videos and endorsements that can be used to garner bigger opportunities. This option is also more on the economical side. Initially, you'll save money on travel costs; and once you create a name for yourself and are able to book bigger events, you may find that the organizations to which you are speaking will cover your travel and expenses, as well as providing an honorarium.

*Know your audience.* Getting to know your audience is just like getting to know any new acquaintance: you have to ask questions to find out what they are all about. Find out in advance what their main concerns are, what challenges they may face, and other unique elements. This will help you to tailor your speech in a way that is engaging and informative for each individual group.

*Get their attention immediately.* It's true what they say about first impressions. If you don't grab your audience's attention from the beginning, there's little hope of keeping them on the edge of their seats for the remainder of your presentation. Think of something to say that is funny, unusual, or even controversial that will hook your audience before you've even really gotten started.

*Tell them "what's in it for them."* Ask yourself before any speaking gig: *Why does this matter to my audience?* In order to deliver a powerful presentation, you have to focus on giving the audience something that they care about, something that is important to them, and a solid reason to care about what you are saying.

*"Listen" to what your audience is telling you.* You're not alone if you've ever found yourself speaking to a room full of people, and you just *knew* it wasn't going well. It happens to the best of the best, and knowing how to handle it will set you apart. "Listen" to any nonverbal feedback your audience may be giving you. For example, do they look bored or disconnected? Paying attention to these cues will tell you when it's time to change courses and amp up your efforts. Don't forget to keep them engaged by repeatedly reminding them "what's in it for them." If you notice your audience getting antsy, then it's time to switch gears!

*Get the sale to close itself.* Bottom line: When a speaker delivers a compelling, passionate presentation, the audience will want to do business with them based solely on the connection he or she has made with them.

*Create a memorable experience.* Try to tap into what sets you apart from other speakers. Are you a great storyteller? Do you excel at audience interaction? Whatever it may be, utilize it! Audiences don't easily forget speakers who truly engage through stories, message, solutions, and emotion.

*It's a conversation, not a presentation.* One of the most common mistakes that speakers make is to talk "at" their audience rather than "to" them. Rather than giving a stiff, overly practiced and highly polished presentation, approach your speech the same way you would a one-on-one meeting with a colleague. Your demeanor, manner of speech, and certainly what you have to say shouldn't be any different than a normal conversation. When you are able to perfect this style of speaking, you will find that your audience becomes more engaged and receptive to you and your message. Think of your speech as a dialogue—*not* a monologue.

*Use rhetorical questions.* When giving a speech, it's helpful to utilize phrases such as "Have you ever noticed . . . ?" or "Am I the only one who feels that . . . ?" Rhetorical questions like these encourage the audience members to really think about what you've said and relate it to a similar experience in their own lives. It will connect them to you in a way that makes them feel as though you understand their concerns and interests on a more personal level.

## Organizing a Great Presentation

There are three distinct sections to any powerful presentation. Whether you are giving a five-minute introduction or an all-day presentation, consider using the "Challenge-Solution-Call to Action" Method:

- Address the *Challenge*
- Form Your *Solution*
- Give the Audience a *Call to Action*

Just like everything else in business, you have to choose the path that's right for you and your company. Some events are better for large corporations, while others are more effective for those who run a small business. But whatever you choose, make sure that you are dedicated to your efforts and see them through to the end. Learn from mistakes and seek out ideas for your own events when you attend others.

Whatever you do—don't give up! If an event isn't profitable for you one year, don't swear them off altogether. Instead, try something new! If nothing else, consider it a way to connect with others—be they clients, future customers, or colleagues. Rest assured that your hard work will pay off; and the connections you make through your events will prove to be priceless.

## Take 15 and Get Your Clients Going Wild!
### A 15-Minute Client-Builder Exercise

What events will you plan this year? Create your event calendar.

_____

_____

_____

_____

_____

# Media Methods to Gain Celebrity Status

## Take Advantage of Hot Topics, Timely Events, and Unique Twists to Attract Attention

T he word "celebrity" tends to conjure images of red carpets, paparazzi, beautiful people, and the Hollywood Hills. However the definition of a celebrity is simply someone who is well-known or famous within a society. You don't have to star in movies or be a professional athlete to earn the title.

Gaining celebrity status in your field, industry, and beyond can play an integral part in building a flourishing business. It allows you to establish yourself as the expert of choice for the media, defines your brand, and most importantly, increases your exposure, thus creating new business opportunities and ways to optimize your success.

There are a variety of methods for achieving celebrity status, but whether you choose to hire a publicist or tackle the task on your own, consider the following questions first:

*What do I bring to the table?* Too many people have fuzzy impressions of who they *really* are and what they *really* do for others. If you don't know, you certainly can't expect others to know. Before you start your celebrity push, make sure you know exactly what service, product, or expertise you provide that no one else can.

*Can I become an expert?* Those of you who aren't Academy Award winners or all-star athletes gain celebrity status by being an expert in your respective field—and then letting people know about it. This chapter will show you some ways to get your name out there.

*How can I make a name for myself?* If you want people to know who you are, then consider creating a persona for yourself. Think of a catchy name that summarizes your area of expertise. Are you a numbers guru? A marketing magician? Think of a name that will attract attention and will be easy to remember. This is also a great way for you to use your expertise in different markets.

Interested? Then read on to discover how to reach celebrity status.

## Go Public!

"Public relations" is one of those terms with meanings that many people find hard to pin down. But what it means for you—in your quest to establish yourself in your industry and beyond—is finding ways to work with the media to get your message out to the public. By working directly with the media or hiring PR professionals to do this for you, you can get information about your latest and greatest successes out to the public. Public relations pros can provide your market with relevant and beneficial information and can use repeated coverage to clear out some space for you in the public's collective psyche—all without your spending gazillions on advertising!

That said—the following initial steps help get you going in the right direction.

*Become a local celebrity first.* Although national media attention is great, consider getting your celebrity feet wet in your hometown first. All celebrity has to start somewhere, and there's no better place to start than in your own back yard.

You can begin by developing a relationship with your local newspaper. Send them regular press materials and updates aimed at garnering quality coverage and getting your name out there. Consider pitching yourself for an interview with your local TV or radio news affiliates as well.

To get the attention of the news media, you must first do something newsworthy. So get involved with local organizations and events that may be of interest to the people in your area. For example, you might sponsor a local sports team or event. Make sure that your name or your organization's name is prominently displayed. Exhibit your wares or promote your services at local events like career fairs, festivals, and charitable events, and do something fun to attract attention and interest—sponsor a raffle, contest, or giveaway to draw people to your booth.

If nothing else, this will provide a great opportunity to "test the waters" at being a media maven in a smaller market. You'll also collect great media clips that you can use to pitch yourself to bigger networks and outlets.

*Go national.* Let's face it—media opportunities aren't just going to show up at your doorstep. You have to do a little legwork first to let people know what you are all about. A great way to gain access to national-level reporters is to subscribe to "story source" services—like ProfNet, which is fee-based, or a free service such as Help A Reporter Out (HARO). Reporters use these tools to find expert sources for stories. They send out a query along with their deadline and contact information, and then it's up to you to respond. All it takes is one big hit to get yourself on the road to celebrity status, so pitch yourself for these stories as frequently as possible to make your way into the national media.

*Go pro.* If you really want to go all out in your quest for media celebrity-hood, you might consider hiring a PR firm. Although you assume that a publicist isn't in your budget, think about this: Successful PR means getting results, and that requires a significant investment of time and energy—so much time and energy that you probably won't be able to do it all yourself. In addition to the time you spend writing (and that's assuming you are a great writer, or already have one on your staff), you must expend some effort developing and managing media lists, as well as making follow-up calls. And if your campaign is a success, you then have to find time to squeeze in interviews and appearances. The point is that if you can't spend the time to do the job right, then you probably want to hire a PR firm that can fulfill some of these duties for you and help you throw your net a little wider.

If you just don't have the budget, you can take a "do-it-yourself" approach. Read on to learn more about this method.

## It Starts with a Compelling Angle

Contrary to what you may think, publicity doesn't have to be expensive. Learn how to craft a decent press release that is both timely and well-written, which can create a lot of bang for your buck—and if you're looking to up your celebrity status, this is a great place to start. It doesn't matter if your initial approach is smaller scale with local media, or if you send your material over the national wire. Either way, a press release can garner big results: from blogs and web sites, to daily newspapers and drive-time radio—even television spots. All it takes is a compelling angle, a catchy headline, and quality content—and you are on the road to getting your name in the press and securing your status as a bona fide media celebrity.

*Begin with an idea.* The first step to creating a great press release is to think like a publicist. If all your release does is announce a new product or service, it doesn't provide the media with any incentive to run your story or article. The media doesn't care about it, and you must remember that *they* are your first audience.

So think about how you can make the editor's job easier when you begin to craft your release. If you provide a newsworthy angle or address a problem that many people face, then editors can use that information in their own articles—or even use your entire release. The trick is to figure out how to transform your particular expertise, product, or service into a story that people will care about, and use that as the springboard for your ideas.

*Plug into a news angle.* Whether you are sending out a press release, launching a new product or coming up with your next big marketing scheme—you can't just put the information out there and expect the media or potential customers to bite. You have to make you, your product, and your organization both relevant *and* current. Pay attention to the news, and especially to the stories that may currently be captivating the country. If you've never been a news junkie before, now is the time to tune in. There may be some hot topics relevant to you that are hiding in those general interest stories; and while some will have obvious tie-ins to your company or service, you may have to get creative with others.

For example, if you are a real estate agent, you might send out a release that speaks to the first-time buyer housing credit. You can provide pertinent statistics and any advice you may have based on your own expertise. Or, say you are a leadership expert, and have heard about a recent survey that's revealed that quality leadership is the most effective way to grow a business during a down economy. Kicking off your press release with those statistics will allow you to provide timely and essential information or advice about your services.

*Bottom line.* Having a newsworthy angle makes it more likely that media outlets will pick up your story, and will make you a bigger celebrity in the process. Some other press release angles to consider:

- Take a seasonal angle.
- Solve a problem.
- Connect to a trend or "emotion."
- Glam up your topic.
- Write for different demographics.

*Grab them with your headline.* The old adage might discourage you from judging a book by its cover, but members of the media will not hesitate to judge a press release by its headline. They are conditioned to decide whether something is worth reading by glancing at the headline. It doesn't matter how well-written or interesting the subject matter is—if you don't have a sexy headline to draw people in, your release is dead in the water.

When you brainstorm on headlines for your releases, consider the things that capture *your* attention when you read articles or browse online. What is it about those particular headlines that catch your eye? Use your headline in a similar way to hook readers from the get-go. Here are four examples of headlines I used for press releases for my first book, *The Connectors*:

1. The "Connection" Key: Seven Ways the World's Most Successful Businesspeople Trounce the Competition—and How You Can, Too

2. 'Tis the Season to Connect: Four Ways to Up Your Networking Ante at This Year's Holiday Parties

3. Connecting Through Conflict: Five Ways Great Connectors Turn Angry Clients into Happy Ones . . . and How You Can, Too!

4. The ABCs of Raising Kid "Connectors": Five Lessons in Connecting that Will Set Your Kids Up for Success Now and in the Future

Not only does each headline clearly state the subject matter in a clever way, it also promises to help the reader solve a problem. This will pique readers'—and even more importantly, editors'—interests. It makes their job easier, which makes it much more likely that your release will get *lots* of pickup!

*Create a media database.* Once your release is ready to go, you need to know where to send it. There are a few ways that you can approach your media list's creation. If you are starting small and local, the best method would be to do a little legwork. Research the phone numbers for your local newspaper, radio, and television stations online, and call to ask their permission to send your press materials. Ask for the appropriate editor or producer to receive your materials, and the best method for sending to them.

If you want to go bigger than your hometown, you may want to consider buying a list. There are several services—such as Cision and BurrellesLuce—that sell media lists and access to media contact information. If you intend to send out several releases over the course of the year, then you might consider a plan that offers a one-year subscription. Or, if your budget is tight and you want to see how well this approach works before you make a long-term commitment, you can opt to buy a single, tailored list. Research the best option before you make a decision.

It's possible that you may make some media contacts on your own, or even by chance. Create a database of media with whom you have made contact—as well as those who have given you permission to send your materials—so that you can send them your press releases. In this instance, it's a good idea to send the release with a personal note or e-mail rather than sending en masse.

*Maintain your media database.* Once your release goes out, you'll want to keep track of the response it gets. Despite the quality writing, engaging content—and titillating subject matter—there's a good chance that it won't be well-received by everyone. In fact, you may have several people request that you take them off your media list. Be proactive about this. Create a database for all of your unsubscribe requests, and add them to a suppression list to ensure that they no longer receive e-mails from you (see Chapter 14, "Permission-Based Marketing").

Always include a note in your database about any requests from reporters to only be contacted regarding certain topics, and only contact them if you are indeed sending related materials. You may also want to add other reminders regarding when editors are planning to use your story, or when a radio producer mentioned he would like to get in touch about a future booking. Staying on top of your media database is an important part of creating your celebrity status and appropriately dealing with the media.

*Submitting your release.* The editorial calendar is a vital consideration when you're dealing with print media. (See Figure 18.1 for an example.) At the beginning of each year, most newspaper and magazine outlets create a plan for the content they intend to cover in the year ahead. Knowing these schedules ahead of time can make it much easier for you to create stories that will interest them, and to pitch yourself and your press release at the right time to increase your chances of success. If you have an established relationship with an editor or reporter, you may simply be able to ask about the calendar, and whether you can have access to it. If not, then you may have to do some searching yourself.

Some newspapers and magazines will post their editorial calendars online on their web sites. A simple web search will help you to find these by searching the publications name or by visiting the individual sites you're interested in. Another trick is to look for the section of the site asking for interested advertisers, because they often need to know the editorial schedule in order to plan their ad campaigns around the publication's content. If all else fails, you can send an e-mail or make a phone call to the publication itself and ask.

A word of caution: Be careful *when* you send your press releases. The best days for submitting this material are Tuesdays through Thursdays. And always avoid submitting releases on the days immediately before and after holidays.

| Month | Theme of Issue | Features | Related Trade Shows/Seminars |
|---|---|---|---|
| January | Getting Off to a Good Start | | |
| February | Bringing In New Business | How to Make New and Lasting Connections | |
| March | Going Tech Savvy | Business By the (Face)Book: How Social Networking Is Changing the Way We Do Business | |
| April | Tax Time | What You Need to Know about Paying Taxes this Year | Last-Minute Tax Advice Webinar— April 2 |
| May | Leadership Lessons | | |
| June | Keeping Employees Happy | | ACME Biz Annual Conf.—June 15–18 |
| July | Networking | | Network Yourself Business Seminar July 12 |
| August | Back to Business School | Why Continuing Ed Is a Good Decision | |
| September | The Economy and Your Business | | |
| October | Marketing Madness | | |
| November | Counting Your Business Blessings | | Better Business Seminar Nov. 4 |
| December | Looking Forward to New Year | | |

**Figure 18.1    Sample Business Magazine Editorial Calendar**

## The Nuts and Bolts of Creating a Great Press Release

*General appearance.* No press release should go out to the media without the following information: your complete contact information including an e-mail address and phone number where the media can reach you; your bio; your web site; a dateline that includes the month and year the release is going out, as well as the city and state of origin. Your release's main body should be in Times New Roman 12 point font, though you can make your headlines bigger and bolder—Times New Roman Bold, 14 point font, for example—to draw attention.

*Appropriate length.* You don't want your press release to be too long, because most reporters are working on limited word counts for their articles and don't have time to read through eight pages of information. A good rule of thumb is to make the release between one and four pages. However, the better the content, the longer your release can be. If you have an abundance of exciting or extremely relevant information to include, your release can spill over the four-page limit. Just make sure that what you are providing is significant, timely, and well-written.

*Style.* As I mentioned earlier, the easier you make it for the media, the more likely they'll be to pick up your release. Style your press release like a traditional news story, with a catchy headline, solid introduction, quotes, and tips. This will increase the chances that your piece will be noticed and run. Feature-style writing—similar to that used in most popular magazines—is usually the best way to grab the reader's attention, and, as a result, is the best way to appeal to many editors. Basically, colorful, compelling writing that paints a picture works better than dry, just-the-facts writing—every time.

*Use quotes.* A great way to convey information in a press release is through quotes, and even though you may be the one creating the release, there's no reason you can't quote yourself! Imagine that you're interviewing yourself on the content of the release, and think about how you would answer certain questions regarding the content. Then include your answers as pithy quotes within your release. Reporters in need of sources for stories will often pull quotes directly from well-written, on-topic press releases.

*Proofread, proofread . . . proofread!* Be sure that you are sending your release out in tip-top shape, so that newspapers and magazines that might be interested can run it easily with little work from their in-house staff. Typos and grammatical errors are the quickest way to get your release completely ignored and your credibility ruined.

*Following up.* So your materials have gone out, but your inbox is empty (except for all those pesky "unsubscribes"!), and your phone is silent. What do you do? Your first instinct may be to call immediately to follow up, but you need to resist that urge and wait it out a bit. Most members of the media receive hundreds of daily contacts from people just like you. In addition to their own jobs' demands, they have to spend time sifting through hundreds of e-mails and voice mails with pitches and story ideas (this is also another great reason why it's so important for your release to stand out).

It's possible that the recipients won't get to your press release today, or even tomorrow, so give them some time to respond. Wait at least three days before following up once your material goes out. This gives reporters ample time to have received and reviewed your materials. And don't be surprised if they say they never saw your release. Simply offer to resend it to them, and make another follow-up call in a day or two.

*Here's an added tip*. When you resend press materials as part of a follow-up, paste your release in the body of the e-mail as well as attaching the actual document. Most recipients prefer not to open attachments in order to avoid potential computer viruses. It also provides reporters or producers fast access to your materials with just a quick scan of their e-mail—especially for those who might be checking their e-mail on their PDA.

## Become a Media Maven

Your level of success is often directly connected to whom you know. Just as your business relationships can help you close that big deal or get the heads up on a great new hire, your media connections will help you get ahead as you strive to become the King or Queen of your field.

Read on to see how you can use your media contacts to quickly leverage yourself to superstar status.

*Connect with the media*. Before you worry about building relationships, you have to make the initial connections. Here's a great trick for those just starting out: think of five reporters you respect. Make a point to regularly read their work, post positive comments on any stories that are posted online, submit editorials about them; or even just send them an e-mail or send a short note with positive feedback about their stories, telling them how much you appreciate their personal writing style and point of view. Then, when you begin your own media push, the feedback you've been giving will pay off. It increases the likelihood that those specific reporters will recognize your name and just might include you in a story. Who knows? As your relationship with them and your media maven status continues to grow, you just might become a go-to source for those reporters.

*Don't be afraid to call*. Just like you, reporters and producers are busy people. Their days are typically fast-paced and jam-packed, and they don't have time to return every e-mail or comment on every release you send out. Don't let the fear of "bothering" a reporter hold you back from picking up the phone. When handled correctly, phone calls are great ways to pitch story ideas or to touch base on press materials you've already sent out.

Keep in mind when making calls that these reporters and producers have full schedules. If you are calling to pitch a story idea, always ask if they have time to listen after you introduce yourself. If they say no, leave it at that. If you think they will genuinely have an interest in your pitch or press release, send it to them in an e-mail. And if you are calling to follow up on something you've already sent, clearly state that is what you are doing at the beginning of the call. Nine times out of 10, though, you'll probably get voicemail, so get a concise, informative pitch or message ready to go as soon as you hear the beep.

*Coordinate your publicity push with your travel schedule.* Every time you travel—whether it's for business or pleasure—is another chance for you to reach a new market and connect with different members of media. Use your trips as an opportunity to send out a new release, or resend an older one. Mention at the beginning that you will be traveling to that particular area, and provide the dates of your visit. Research the region's local media and make some phone calls ahead of time. Let reporters and producers know that you'll be around, and would love to do some interviews. And most importantly, research the area and demographic before you start pitching yourself. Tailor your expertise, product, or service to the needs and interests of the territory's residents.

*Interview etiquette.* Again, one of the most effective ways to become a media darling is to make reporters and producers' jobs easier. If a reporter, radio host, or television producer contacts you about an interview, it's important that you follow a few rules of thumb:

### Pre-Interview

- *Call back immediately.* If a reporter contacts you for an interview (and you miss the call), call them back *immediately*. Most reporters are working on a deadline, so if they're not able to connect with you right away, they will move on to another source.

- *Be available.* This may mean investing in a dedicated phone line for media to call and having a reliable voice-mail and e-mail system as well as perhaps call-waiting. If you get a reputation for being difficult to reach, the media will pass over your name when looking for a source.

- *Work on the reporter's schedule.* Again, bear in mind that just like you, reporters are busy people who are working against tight deadlines every single day. If a reporter wants to talk to you at 9 PM one evening or on a Saturday afternoon—*do it*. They'll appreciate your willingness to be flexible, and will remember it the next time around.

- *Be prepared.* Once you have an interview on the books, re-familiarize yourself with the subject matter (regardless of how well you think you know it). Conduct some additional research on the topic, create some interesting talking points, and read up on the publication so that you can prepare for the reporter's or producer's audience. Have any notes in front of you during the interview so that you can refer back to them when necessary and you can keep the conversation flowing.

## During the Interview

- *Speak in sound bites.* In other words, be easy to quote. Convey your information as concisely and directly as possible. It increases your chances of being directly quoted in a story, and it makes it more likely that portions of your interview will be rerun for radio and television interviews.

- *Remember that nothing is ever "off the record."* Don't let yourself get too comfortable when you are speaking to a reporter. Even if the reporter begins to speak on a personal matter themselves, remind yourself that nothing you say is ever off the record. There's nothing more stomach-turning than seeing something you didn't mean to say show up in ink in a major publication.

- *Don't be defensive.* The media are natural antagonists, and often play the devil's advocate in order to get all sides of a story. It's what makes them good at what they do, and what generates compelling interviews and great stories. If you are challenged during an interview, don't let it get to you. Remain calm and stick to the talking points. Getting angry will only cost you good media coverage and a valuable relationship—and will likely cause you to say something you don't want in print or on the air.

- *Be accurate.* Again, remember that the information you provide is going to show up somewhere and that many people out there are ready to scrutinize what you say. Be sure that your material is accurate, and check and double-check any numbers or statistics. If you want to use data to back up a point, make sure it's right. And certainly don't dole out any advice that isn't sound. Your credibility is at stake!

## Post-Interview

- *Send a thank-you note.* The same rules that you follow after a job interview apply here: Once your interview is over, send a *hand-written* thank-you note to the reporter, producer, or host who coordinated and/or conducted it. Thank the person for thinking of you and tell him or her how much you enjoyed the interview. Emphasize that you would *love* to be a source again in the future.

- *Ask when the story will run, and if you can have the clip when it does.* One of the biggest mistakes people make when it comes to media is failing to check on a story's status after they have been interviewed. Most of the time, reporters and producers will be more than happy to provide a run date for your interview, and in many cases, will even give you a hard copy of the print clip or a CD or DVD recording of your appearance. These clips can be extremely valuable when it comes to creating your press kit.

*Google yourself.* When you send information about yourself out into the media world—whether it's via press release, media kit, or interview—there's a good chance that certain media outlets will use it, or quote you and never let you know. Conducting a simple Google search of your name, your company's name, or your product or service can reveal media placement that you didn't even know you had. It may also reveal negative reviews or other less-than-positive press that you'll want to know about.

*Leverage your media clips.* Once you have your clips in hand, it's important that you know how to use them. First and foremost, create a media page on your web site. Keep it up-to-date with links to any articles you have done, sound clips of radio interviews, and video clips of television appearances. Keep a running memo with any places where you have been featured—including each outlet's logo and circulation—and include it in any press kits or media packages you send out. Packaging your clips in this way will be a huge asset when booking speaking engagements.

Additionally, most television stations—particularly the big ones—will want to see clips of previous interviews before they will book you. Once they see how experienced you are, they will be much more likely to come to you for interviews time and again.

## Put It in Writing

Extra, extra! Television and radio are certainly great methods of gaining exposure, but there is something dignified about having your name, expertise, and viewpoints featured in print. Not only will it position you as an expert to the press, you'll be a star in your clients' (and potential clients') eyes as well.

*Write a book.* Although the thought of writing a book may seem a bit daunting at first, you should consider giving authorship a go. You probably have enough experience—both personal and professional—to fill the pages of a book with valuable information. You can use your book (or books) to establish yourself as an expert in your given field, and therefore as a way to promote yourself in the media and to leverage other opportunities, like speaking.

*Create a white paper.* A white paper is an innovative, if unconventional, way to market yourself and establish your expertise. White papers present factual, well-thought-out arguments and information based on a given product or service, and usually portray the product or service as a solution to a problem. They commonly include studies or other research to back up the arguments they make. White papers go out to potential customers, industry thought leaders and insiders, and any other key influencers within a given industry or field.

Make sure that your white paper immediately identifies the problem it is trying to solve, makes a compelling argument, and details a topic that your reader cares about. Post it on your web site or include it with a complementing press release. To learn how to get started with your white paper, go to www.stelzner.com/copy-HowTo-whitepapers.php.

*Write an op-ed.* One great way to make a name for yourself in the media is to write a compelling op-ed piece. Pay attention to potentially controversial or media-friendly stories and issues that tie into your field or area of expertise. You'll surely have an opinion on the subject matter, so voice it! Make sure that anything you submit is well-written, thoughtful, and makes a compelling case. And don't limit yourself to just one. If there is something out there that you want to say—then say it. Just be prepared to defend yourself and your opinions.

*Write articles.* Celebrity cannot be achieved through press releases alone. Make yourself available to write articles for trade publications that are specific to your industry, as well as for magazines and newspapers that have general audiences. Not only is it great exposure for you today, but thanks to the Internet and search engines like Google, these articles will spread the word about you online for years and years to come.

*Create and distribute a survey or sponsor a poll . . . then report the results.* Surveys are a great way to garner media attention. Try to think about yours from a press release standpoint as you create it. Use questions that you can tie directly to your product, service, or area of expertise. Consider hiring a company to conduct a survey for you, or do it yourself if you have the right resources, then use it as a springboard for a series of press releases or articles.

The same goes for sponsoring a poll. News media love to report on polls, and feature them regularly. Think of ways that you can tie the poll with your expertise so that you can use it to leverage yourself with the media.

## Put All the Pieces Together

The following is an example of a particular company's efforts to make it-self known in the media: Company X is a recognized leader in creating productive workplace cultures that are filled with passionate, dedicated people who are committed to increasing market share, building brand value, embracing new ideas, and delivering superior customer service. They created a variety of surveys to showcase how unhealthy workplace cultures were and gave advice as to what companies should do about it.

All the survey questions were related to company culture, reinforcing Company X as the expert on this subject. Company X released its findings through a series of press releases and tip sheets:

*Press Release*

"Survey Shows That One in Five Employees Plans to Quit Their Job to Pursue a More Balanced Life"

*A new research study reveals that 18 percent of workers plan to leave their jobs within the next year to improve their work-life balance. Company X reflects on this "early warning" and offers advice to aid in fixing of company culture.*

*Tip Sheet: Five Ways to Help Your Employees Create a Healthy Work/Life Balance*

*Press Release*

"The Overwhelmed Office: Six Fixes for the Stressed-Out, Productivity-Challenged Workplace"

New survey suggests one in five workers may be overwhelmed by stress. Company X offers some solutions for diffusing stress in your company and ratcheting up productivity.

## Now Submit!

If you haven't figured it out by now, reaching celebrity status can take a lot of hard work, and it's not going to happen overnight. There are many methods for getting your name out there. The trick is to find what works well for you. What you must understand is that celebrity status is the sum of all of these parts. There's no silver bullet that's going to shoot you straight to the top. All of your efforts will work together to help you gain momentum in your quest for celebrity-dom, and often *you'll* have to connect the dots and make it happen. So, for example, if you are featured as an expert in an article, it's your job to tweet about it, post the link on Facebook, use the clip in promotional materials, and follow up with the reporter in hopes that you'll be featured in a future story.

In an age where new minor celebrities pop up every day, it's vital that you establish yourself as person of substance with great staying power. You have to build a solid foundation for your celebrity to stand on. And once you are able to do that—and do it well—the rest will fall into place.

---

### Take 15 and Get Your Clients Going Wild!
### *A 15-Minute Client-Builder Exercise*

What press releases or articles could you write? How many will you commit to this year?

_____

_____

_____

_____

# Special Tactics for Financial Advisors

## Ten Specific Strategies Working Today

*Red Zone Marketing has worked with thousands of financial advisors and firms in the financial services industry since 1994. The following is a summary of what we have observed to be working best right now to build small and large financial services practices—and truly get clients wildly delighted about their financial professional.*

### How Does One Advisor Really Stand Out from the Others?

Being a financial advisor has been rated as one of the best jobs for 2010.[1] Although that's good news for the industry, it means that there will be even more individuals joining the current lineup of brokers, financial advisors, financial planners, insurance agents, and banking and credit union financial professionals. Clients tend to look around and see "experts" everywhere. Therefore, the key for any advisor today is to find a way to stand out and differentiate from the rest in an increasingly crowded marketplace.

One potential differentiator is the relationship that an advisor has with his or her current clients. The financial services business is, ultimately, a relationship business. There is a direct correlation between the acquisition of referrals and the bonds that advisors form with their clients. Some clients are so impressed with the connection they've made that they simply *want* to introduce their advisor to their friends, family, and colleagues.

Your current clients will tell you what your differentiation is, so ask or formally survey them. If, however, you receive responses that are not that compelling, you may have to stop and figure out a new way of standing out as the extraordinary advisor that you really are. (See sample survey in Figure 19.1.)

---

### Sample Survey Questions to Ask Clients to Determine Your Differentiation

1. How would you currently describe our organization to someone else who may have a need for our services?

    _____

    _____

    _____

    _____

2. How have you described our organization in the past?

    _____

    _____

    _____

    _____

    On a scale of 1–5 with 5 being the best . . .

3. We keep you fully informed.              ⑤ ④ ③ ② ①

4. We do things right the first time.        ⑤ ④ ③ ② ①

5. We are focused on quality
   personal service.                          ⑤ ④ ③ ② ①

6. We regularly provide information
   of value.                                  ⑤ ④ ③ ② ①

7. We have adequate contact with you. ⑤ ④ ③ ② ①

8. Our employees go above and beyond ⑤ ④ ③ ② ①
   for you.

   *Does any employee in particular stand out here?*

   _____

   _____

   _____

   _____

9. We make it easy for you to contact us. ⑤ ④ ③② ①

10. I would be willing to recommend your services to a friend or
    colleague. Yes/No

    *And here's a referral right now!*

**Figure 19.1    Sample Survey for Clients**

## So, What's Working?

This section describes some marketing strategies that many of the most
successful advisors in the United States use successfully. And although
many of these may be common—or common sense—approaches, they are
without a doubt the tactics that—when performed well and with consistency—have produced consistent sales growth, valuable relationships, and
a higher than average number of referrals.

### 1.   *Become the Media*

One of the most powerful ways to gain exposure, increase your
credibility, and get people talking is to get media coverage. This can be
difficult to do on a regular basis, though, and compliance departments often are resistant to advisors being interviewed on TV or radio because
they are unable to control the message as tightly as they'd like. But one
way to get media exposure—and allow compliance to maintain over-
sight—is to host your own recorded radio show. In essence, you *become*

the media, and you can do so by using some newer tools that are available for free and right from your desk.

Thanks to the magic of online media these days, you don't have to work for a communications company or in broadcasting to be an on-air personality. One popular resource is web-based company Blog Talk Radio (www.blogtalkradio.com), which hosts Internet talk radio shows that anyone can use easily—and for free. The only things you need are a computer and a phone.

This online radio show format also makes it simple to share your broadcast through your online social networks. You can archive the shows online so that your listeners can download or listen to them whenever they like—unlike traditional radio where they probably aren't going to hear you at all if they did not hear your program's original recording. I personally use this tool to share valuable business-building ideas by interviewing authors, CEOs, and other professional thought leaders. It is a unique way to extend your brand and communicate with other experts, prospects, and advocates.

By linking to your shows from your web site, clients can listen online live or to archived recordings; they can even download your material to their iPods or other portable devices. The people you interview will usually be interested and flattered to be on your show; and this approach makes it easy to send your broadcasts to compliance, and edit the recordings if required.

There are countless advantages to employing Blog Talk Radio to enhance your brand. One example of someone who makes it work is an advisor I know who uses this tool to reach out to people with whom he wants to develop business contacts. He's interviewed an owner of a large paving and infrastructure company; a business attorney; the owner of an advertising agency; a chiropractor that just opened a new office; the chief economist for the U.S. Department of Agriculture; the owner of a multi-location pizza franchise; and the owner of a large emerging market food GPO. He gives each interviewee the recorded file of their interactions, so that they can use it in their own marketing plans as well. "Everyone [we] approached did not hesitate to say yes. Talk about an overwhelming response. It was like shooting fish in a barrel!" said Chuck Hammond, CMFC, with RRG, Inc.

You can also create and promote your own series of video interviews by setting up a webcam and using Skype (www.Skype.com), along with an onscreen recording program like Jing (www.jingproject.com). This allows you to easily perform video interviews without any costly phone bills, and it's a great way to get some face-to-face time with those with whom you want to continue building relationships. These videos can easily be updated to your web site, blog, and YouTube channel.

You'll find that most people you approach will be flattered and more than happy to grant an interview; and another benefit is that you will have permanently formed a connection with a potentially powerful advocate or prospect. By promoting the interview via LinkedIn and through your network, you can get a lot of exposure from fellow businesspeople—as well as from potential and current clients.

## 2. Yes, Seminars Are Working!

*Public seminars and social events.* Many people have written off seminars as an expensive strategy that hasn't been as successful as a few years ago. But the truth is that they are still working!

According to advisors who conduct large dinner seminars, the response rates are up, sometimes double the 2008 numbers.

"After a period of a market downturn—after 9/11 and the beginning of 2009—we have seen activity levels rise with advisors placing mailing orders and also a rise in seminar attendance," said Jorge Villar, President of Response Mail Express, a seminar marketing firm in Tampa, Florida. "Consumers are looking to learn about newer options, alternate solutions, and trends."

*Referral-based seminars.* A low-risk, low-cost seminar strategy that has worked in the past and continues to succeed is the niche-based referral seminar. One approach that's currently being used is called the "5-5-5-20" seminar, where you pick five or more of your clients that are members of a particular "niche" (for example, they have all retired from the same company). Mail each client five invitations to an upcoming workshop on a seminar with a topic, like: *How to Retire from* [local company] *in Volatile Market Conditions*. Then make personal phone calls to the five clients and ask them to pass those invitations along to others who are getting ready to retire from the company. This strategy typically generates more than 20 attendees per seminar. It costs little (about $2 for the whole mailing), targeted invitees are interested in the event topic, and you don't even need to serve dinner! Advisors are conducting these seminars at community centers, libraries, and even in their offices. Many have been utilizing this inexpensive, highly effective seminar method to produce qualified, targeted prospects and clients. In fact, some have built their entire careers on this low-cost strategy.

*Presentations for existing groups.* There has also been increased interest in having financial professionals speak at meetings of groups and organizations lately. One advisor is an active member of his large Chamber of Commerce, and has been asking for years to speak at one of the Chamber's monthly luncheons. Though he was told "no" repeatedly, because of the heightened awareness of the financial services industry these days, he is receiving newly enhanced interest from groups in his community to have him speak. He went to his Chamber just recently and mentioned a presentation he had designed called, "What *Not* to Do with Your Money Now." They cancelled their previously scheduled speaker and put him on the agenda as the main speaker. Have times changed! Now, people really *do* want to hear you.

### 3.   One-on-One "Seminars"

Another strategy that's enjoying some recognition is a brand new concept in the seminar business called "Concierge Consultation." This approach—developed by Response Mail—recognizes that while seminars continue to be the most effective, cost-per-lead form of lead generation, a growing number of advisors are looking for other cost-efficient and cost-effective options to group dinner seminar events. In addition, there is a large segment of the population that either will not respond to a traditional seminar invitation, or is uncomfortable discussing financial matters in a group setting.

This strategy is designed to be a one-on-one seminar that uses the best elements of traditional event marketing—and allows an advisor to get in front of a qualified prospect. Advisors send out a seminar-like invitation—based on age and income—to a selected group of people. Prequalification questions are designed to make sure that the most eligible clients are being encouraged to schedule one-on-one dinner appointments. People who respond to the mailing are prequalified by a call center, and then arrange a dinner meeting with the advisor. The system basically puts advisors in front of fully qualified prospects who want to meet with them in a more personal, one-to-one atmosphere.

"I am getting about 20 appointments per mailing [by] using this strategy," said Jon Butenuth, an advisor from Illinois who is ranked in the top 10 at his broker dealer. "The prospects are prequalified, so the only thing I have been concerned with is focusing their need for *my* services. I am actually holding the meetings at lunch, which is less expensive than dinner. It really lets me do my job and not have to be a marketer."

## 4. Referrals—Receiving Without Asking!

Have you ever sat through a workshop designed to improve your referral generating skills? Did you develop your script, role-play with others, ask yourself if you're referable, and so forth? Although this exercise can be extremely valuable for acquiring referrals, the reality is that most financial advisors would rather *not* ask; and so, this is not done with consistency. After all, you put off doing most things that you don't feel comfortable doing—at least for a period of time. For that reason, I want to share two proven referral-generating strategies that *don't* require asking, because ultimately, receiving recommendations is about the way you make clients feel—and how often that happens with positive results.

1. *Don't Miss the Boat:* One of the most successful strategies I've seen for giving clients a reason to immediately refer is an event called, "Don't Miss the Boat." It's similar to a client-appreciation event, but the only people invited are those clients who have referred others to your firm. It has consistently produced referrals of 40 or more per event—even from high net-worth individuals! (This event has been fully detailed in Chapter 11, "Your Best Prospects Come from Referrals.")

2. *The Fuel Card:* The manner in which you thank clients who refer can actually generate even *more* customers. If you send a small gift that the referrer can use *right away*, it will prompt those same clients to give more referrals. For example—if you send a $20 fuel card as a referral thank you—when do you think clients will use it? Right away! And who do you think they'll be thinking of when they use it? You! Most of your good clients want to recommend you to others—they may just need a friendly reminder. This fuel card provides them with an immediate reminder of you.

## 5. Charity Alliances

One advisor in California has taken a different path for developing the often-elusive referrals from centers of influence like CPAs, lawyers, and P&C agencies. This individual—who only works with high net-worth folks—has begun focusing on his involvement in charitable events and causes. He began to employ this method during the recent market downturn of late 2008 into 2009. Though he had traditionally held a gala client appreciation dinner at his house every year, he decided that February 2009 might not have been the wisest time to be celebrating. He wanted to wait until the market recovered, so he decided instead to offer the same date to a charity to do a fundraiser for *them*. The charity was obviously thrilled and incredibly grateful—and began by handing the advisor a list of the charity's top donors to invite them to his event.

The advisor designed a simple invitation for the fundraiser and sent the invites via e-mail to his clients, prospects, community leaders, and the charity-provided donor list. He then also placed phone calls to personally invite people on the list. During calls with charity donors, he discussed the organization's status—and also asked if they wanted to go out to lunch sometime in the future to discuss how they might help the nonprofit. He then followed up a day later with a specific date for lunch.

The advisor gave a brief presentation at the event about what the charity meant to him. He also had a few of the big donors and someone from the organization speak. The whole presentation took about 35 minutes.

The fundraiser was a winning situation for everyone involved. It allowed the advisor to develop many new relationships with high net-worth individuals; it enabled the charity to raise thousands of dollars in a difficult period ($10,000 on the night of the event alone); and the advisor's eventual new investment clients turned 2009 into one of his best years in the business.

## 6.   *Your Brand Awareness*

Does your "brand" set you apart from other advisors in your clients' and prospects' eyes? Top advisors often have a strong brand that can be described simply: *Your brand is what people say about you.* It's *not* your logo, tag line, or elevator speech; it is how someone else describes you, your firm, your staff, and your offerings. And although your brand exists whether you like it or not, you *do* have the power to control it.

Your clients are the leading source for letting you know what people think your firm is all about, and you can control your brand through your clients almost entirely through your communication with them. Impactful contact with your clients leads to confidence and trust. It will differentiate you from others, make your clients feel important, give them something to talk about, and bring you the referrals you deserve.

The stronger your brand, the more credible and visible you are, and the easier it becomes for others to do business with you. And in some cases, you may want to work to give them the words to say about you.

# Develop Your 15-Second *Simple, Repeatable Statement of Value* (SRSV)

Answer the following questions:

1. Who are you?

   _____

   _____

   _____

   _____

2. What do you do?

   _____

   _____

   _____

   _____

3. Who specifically do you serve?

   _____

   _____

   _____

   _____

4. What is something unique about you, your business, or those
   with whom you work?

   _____

   _____

   _____

   _____

**Example:** I work with family-owned businesses, helping them
pay less in taxes and protect their assets. I specifically work with
those who have serious profit problems. Big profits.

**Example:** I own a marketing consulting firm that employs six
people, all of whom are focused on helping companies find more
business. I've worked with an NBA basketball team, U.S. Senators,
financial advisors, and mutual fund companies. I've even closed
a sale while upside down in an aerobatic biplane at 3,000 feet
above ground.

## 7.  Your Community Involvement

Being an active member of the community establishes name recognition and positive awareness. It's no coincidence that many top advisors are also involved in their towns and cities. It's almost like magic, but when you give back and develop a positive brand as a good member of the community, business naturally comes your way. One advisor has taken a leadership role in his local Chamber of Commerce. Many advisors don't find success in working with chambers but this advisor attributes 50 percent of his new business in 2009 from his chamber contacts and their network of contacts. He credits his chamber for his high visibility and leadership status that gives all the members a chance to see and get to know him.

## 8.  Your Online Presence Defines You

When a prospect or client searches for you online or arrives at your web site, do they see what they want to see? Does the material provided answer their questions and/or exceed their expectations? Most importantly—does it create a connection between the visitor and the financial services firm?

*Seven seconds to make a great first impression.* Recent statistics indicate that people form an opinion of a web site in seven seconds, and will decide within that time frame whether to browse within your site—or move on. Keeping this in mind, it is important to have a web site design that downloads quickly, is aesthetically pleasing, and tells users right away what's in it for them. Simply put, your site needs to stop visitors in their tracks.

*It's not all about you—it's about them!* Your web site's home page is most effective if it has a clearly stated message specifically aimed at your target market. If, for example, you work with clients who are near or at retirement, then have a box they can click on with "Important Information to Know Before You Retire"; or "Already Retired? Learn the Most Effective Income Preservation Strategies." The visitor will go toward content specifically for them. As we discussed previously, it's all about benefits, not the features.

*Your site should be unique, just like your company.* An attractive model or stock photography on your site does not tell visitors anything much about who you are. You want to let visitors truly get to know your firm. Powerful tools for doing so include pictures of you and your staff; video and audio that uses your voice to tell visitors about your company; and specific commentary about the benefits you provide to your target market.

*Don't forget your call to action.* A web site's success is measured by its "web conversion rate"—the amount of visitors that you convert into customers. You need to nudge prospects to connect with your site so that they eventually take the action you want. Several ways to encourage their interaction is to offer them something of value (free report or newsletter), in exchange for filling out information. Or provide them with an option to request a complimentary retirement analysis or to schedule an appointment.

*Evaluate your site using analytics.* You can use a tool like Google Analytics (www.google.com/analytics) to statistically evaluate your site. This is how you find out if people searched for your site; what key words they used; how long they stayed on your site; where they went when they came upon it; and if they were repeat or new visitors. Use the information to continue to improve your home page and entire site.

### 9. Deliver Your Messages via Video

Meeting with customers face-to-face is vital to earning more referrals, but can often be a difficult task given busy schedules and high numbers of clients. Some advisors have overcome this challenge by delivering messages to prospects and clients via video. Services like AdvisorTLC. com allow them to quickly and easily create and deliver personalized, emotional, and relevant video content to clients—and then send it through e-mail. It can even be sent directly to compliance for their approval before delivery.

You can use video for a number of things—to deliver market updates, provide education, give referral introductions, transmit thank-you messages, and announce special event wishes and product information and updates. Video even allows you to automate the ability to receive more highly qualified referrals. Messages that recognize certain events and dates—birthdays, anniversaries, and so forth—will go out automatically or on a predetermined schedule.

The biggest benefit to using video—beyond crafting a more personalized message—is the ability to go viral. For example, one New Jersey–based advisor has videotaped himself singing "Happy Birthday"—a video that each of his clients' receive via e-mail on their birthdays. He has already counted 14 referrals from clients who have passed it along to their family and friends—which have turned into new business.

### 10. Doing Something Really Out of the Box

Financial advisor and CEO of MarketDominationProgram.com Seth Greene has created a unique package of information for prospects that not only gets them calling to schedule an appointment, it converts into a sale more than 85 percent of the time. But in order to have such results, it must really be something out of the ordinary. Greene's information package—the "Shock & Awe" box—is only sent to qualified prospects who are interested in Seth's services as a financial advisor.

Here's how the program works: People who call in requesting more information are qualified for interest over the phone. Then the Shock & Awe begins when the box is delivered by private messenger service or via FedEx. Greene also suggests "hiring" a spouse or kids (who can drive) to drop it off. Give them a clipboard, and have them make the prospect sign a receipt so it is official—but don't tell the prospect it is coming!

Inside the box (which is really a large Styrofoam cooler) is a welcome page that introduces Greene and his qualifications; a table of contents that describes the box's items; a service guarantee and mission statement; a list of Greene's suite of services; a "Make Smart Choices with Your Money Guide"; Omaha Steaks (an advance referral gift); a referral worksheet; a temporary tattoo with Greene's company name on it (taking a page from Harley-Davidson); a Rolls Royce Limousine Service certificate good for a ride to Greene's office for the client's appointment; a *Forbes Investment Guide* article advising people to pay for a financial plan (from an objective third-party source); Greene's written value proposition; and many more individual articles on financial, estate, and tax planning.

When a qualified prospect gets a box like this, they can hardly ignore it. In fact, as its title suggests, those who receive it often experience a sense of "shock and awe." But most importantly, Greene can directly attribute more than $1,000,000 in fees and commissions to his Shock & Awe box to date. A real "out of the box idea"—with tangible results!

---

## Take 15 and Get Your Clients Going Wild!
### A 15-Minute Client-Builder Exercise

Select one new idea you will implement this year in your marketing.

_____

_____

_____

_____

*Financial advisors who are creating powerful relationships and connections with their clients, prospects, and communities are using these simple strategies consistently to see dramatic results. For free resources and free downloads of additional tools for business planning and planning your marketing, go to www.RedZoneMarketing.com or www.AndtheClientsWentWild.com.*

# NOTES

## Chapter 2

1. "A Business Model VCs Love." Business 2.0. 2006-10-01. http://money.cnn.com/magazines/business2/business2_archive/2006/10/01/8387115/index.htm.
2. De la Iglesia, JLM, and JEL Gayo, "Doing Business by Selling Free Services." *Web 2.0: The Business Model* (New York: Springer, 2008).
3. Tom Hayes, *Jump Point: How Network Culture is Revolutionizing Business.* (McGraw-Hill, 2008), p. 195.

## Chapter 5

1. Article by W. David Bayless, President, Small World Networks, Inc. that appeared in HYPERLINK \\\\hb2\\p&t\\lines\\hline\\Christine\\PROJECTS\\KuzmeskiAndtheClientsWentWild\\www.Score.com \\hb2\p&t\lines\hline\Christine\PROJECTS\Kuzmeski-AndTheClientsWentWild\www.Score.com.
2. Harbison, J.R., Pekar, P. Jr., Viscio, A., and Moloney, D. *The Allianced Enterprise: Breakout Strategy for the New Millennium* (Los Angeles: Booz Allen & Hamilton, 2000). Available from www.boozallen.com.

## Chapter 12

1. Attributed to KT Design & Development, Grayslake, Illinois.

## Chapter 19

1. Yahoo! Education, "Top Jobs for 2010," http://education.yahoo.net/articles/top_jobs_for_2010.htm.

# INDEX